Progressing Through Grief

For general information on our other products and services or to obtain technical support, please contact our Customer Care Department within the United States at (866) 744-2665, or outside the United States at (510) 253-0500.

Althea Press publishes its books in a variety of electronic and print formats. Some content that appears in print may not be available in electronic books, and vice versa.

Author photograph © Sherwood Triart

ISBN: Print 978-1-62315-722-7 | eBook 978-1-62315-723-4

Progressing Through Grief

Guided Exercises to Understand Your Emotions and Recover from Loss

STEPHANIE JOSE, LMHC, LCAT

Foreword by Cécile Rêve, LMHC

ALTHEA
PRESS

Contents

Foreword

Loss touches each of us at some point in our lives—and grief is a normal and natural reaction, no matter how it affects us. I've known grief in different forms. I lost my sister twice: first to schizophrenia, and again when she died. She was diagnosed with this disease following a suicide attempt. I was young and in college, and I felt helpless when confronted with the possibility of her death. I had lost this key person from my life to mental illness, and then she died. Both of these losses caused me great sadness, confusion, anger, and loneliness. Talking about my experience was very difficult because no one around me seemed to understand my complex feelings. What did finally help me overcome my grief was learning about other people's experiences. Some of these experiences came from stories I found in a book, like the one you are holding now. The ability to put myself in somebody else's shoes, to know that others have gone through (and survived) loss, made me feel less alone and hopeful that I would feel "normal" again.

Like Stephanie, I also understand grief from the clinical perspective of a licensed mental health counselor and certified expressive arts therapist. Some of the questions we are often asked include: "Is this normal?" or "Am I going crazy?" *Progressing Through Grief* answers these universal questions and others, and illustrates how personal and unique each person's experience is with loss.

When you grieve, you will likely experience complicated, confusing, and uncomfortable feelings—and in reaction to this, you may feel disconnected from your body. You may have difficulty even with simple daily activities. Both Stephanie and I believe that the healing process involves both the mind and body, and as such, *Progressing Through Grief* offers a reassuring perspective and unique strategies to process your grief and bring your mind and body back into harmony.

The words on the following pages come from Stephanie's years of clinical practice. The wisdom, honesty, and openness with which Stephanie views human emotion are key to why *Progressing Through Grief* is a wonderful tool to get to know more about yourself as you overcome grief. The resourcefulness and humanness she uses to support her clients is present throughout this book, and ready to help you reflect and learn.

Wishing you, with Stephanie as your guide, a smooth transition back to stability and possibilities for the future as your new, wiser, and peaceful self.

—CÉCILE RÊVE, LMHC
Co-founder of ART*relief*, an expressive arts therapy center

Introduction

Twenty years later, I can still remember exactly where I was when I heard the news. It was spring. I was rushing through the halls between classes in high school, trying to get to my locker so I would not have to carry an extra book. Someone walked up from behind me and told me she had killed herself. Suddenly, everything became a blur. Life moved at a slower pace. None of the faces in the hallway seemed familiar. Was this real? It couldn't be—this was my friend, and I had just seen her. She hadn't said anything. Or had she? Was there some clue I had missed?

As the news spread, a teacher stopped her class and gave us the opportunity to talk about what had happened. Surrounded by other people who cared about her, I came out of the haze and realized I was not alone. For a long time though, I blamed myself for not being a better friend and replayed our conversations over and over again believing that I could have changed the outcome. Those feelings lingered, but I found support from others who knew her.

I don't share my experience of loss as a comparison to your own. On the contrary, I believe everyone's experience is extremely personal. Mine, in particular, led me to pursue a career as a therapist. When I started working in the mental health field in 1999, my focus was on grief, loss, and depression. I wanted to understand the different ways that people grieve and what helps them heal. As I moved from acute psychiatric hospitals to outpatient and residential facilities, then finally to private practice, I saw that people encounter common hurdles when it comes to grief. These hurdles include feelings of loneliness, a loss of control over their grief, and an inability to recover from grief, to name a few. But they can all be overcome.

Grieving is a process that does not completely end; it evolves and becomes integrated into your life. What this means is that your loss, and the grief that comes with it, will become a part of who you are, how you see the world, and what you value. It can even help you grow. Although I cannot promise you a time frame in which you will feel better, I can promise that the grief will not weigh on you forever if you allow yourself the opportunity to grieve. Grieving is a normal part of life, and the more we express our grief and not try to hide from it, the easier it becomes to manage. We all have experienced challenges and stressors in our lives, so we all have the ability to cope, heal, and grow with life's experiences. It just takes time to understand what we individually need. This time of your life may be tough, but you *can* get through this.

Your first impulse might be to try to ignore your feelings and get back to your daily life. This simply does not work in the long run. I cannot emphasize enough: Allow yourself the opportunity to grieve. Grieving does not have to be crying for hours, though crying has a very useful place in the process. Grieving can be proactive—there are many things you can do and tools you can use to help you work through grief. One of the tools we will utilize in this book is journaling. This will provide you with the space to explore your thoughts and feelings on your own, without judgment. I will provide you with specific directives or topics to think about. I encourage keeping the journal close to you so that when you think of something important or feel the need for release, you can write about it. Writing out your thoughts makes them less intimidating and more manageable, and lets you work out any emotions you might be feeling. Writing can also stimulate memories, ideas, and inspirations.

This book is divided into three parts. Part 1: Understanding Grief discusses why it is important to grieve, how grief affects your body, and coping skills that can help. Part 2: Emotions and Reactions will help you to understand feelings such as sadness, anger, guilt, anxiety, disbelief, and shame. Finally, Part 3: Journaling through Grief encourages you to jump right in and express what you are feeling. I will provide prompts and the opportunity to journal throughout the book, but part 3 explores journaling in more detail. Note that this is not a book meant to be read from beginning to end, and then set aside. It's meant to be your companion—helping you understand your feelings as they arise and giving you the space to reflect on them.

I hope this book helps you while you are going through this difficult time by providing you with some information, direction, and inspiration to continue healing and growing as you move forward on the sometimes unpredictable, but always promising, journey of life.

—STEPHANIE JOSE, LMHC, LCAT

Author's note: I have included some client stories to help illustrate the different ways grief manifests itself and to explain how we might work through these issues. The names and details have been changed to protect their confidentiality and privacy.

Understanding Grief

Grief is our reaction to a loss; it's our way of healing. We need time to heal, but many of us ignore our personal needs in order to meet the demands of everyday life. We forget to take care of ourselves. Allowing your mind and body to heal after a loss is important—even critical. Just like you would not leave a broken leg without attention, you should not leave an emotional injury unattended. Taking time to stop and breathe, assess how the loss is affecting you, and figure out what you need to move forward will smooth this transition in your life.

Being Open to Grief

Being open to grief means you acknowledge that it's in your life right now, and you are allowing yourself to react however you need to. In doing so, you do not try to avoid it or fit it in a specific mold of what grief should look like. You just accept what you are thinking and feeling. Note that the expectations about how you should typically grieve may not actually be what you experience or need. Losing someone you cared about, even when the loss is expected, can be a shock. When the shock passes, recognition of the loss makes our mind and body feel uneasy and our existence more fragile. It can even throw our values into question.

There is no set course of action to grieve, no prescribed way to feel, so allow yourself the freedom to respond to the loss in whatever ways you need.

Grief Is Healing

Grief is one of the hardest experiences we go through in life. It sneaks up on us at inconvenient times, drains our energy, and leaves us feeling incomplete and without direction. It can be completely overwhelming. When people think about grief, many think of it as a time when they are broken, a phase that they should quickly fix to get back to life. But grief is not quick, nor is it going to let you get back to the life you once knew. After a loss, your life will be different. You will be changed. The healing, however long it takes, will integrate the loss into who you are now becoming. You may look at life and death differently, reassess religious beliefs, or value things that seemed meaningless before (or vice versa). Try as you might, you do not simply get back to life. Grieving is not wasted time, though; it's time you use to connect with your thoughts and feelings to become complete again.

To begin to heal, we must move toward our grief. We must experience it, express it, and be honest about it. Allow it to come out, however messy or irrational it may seem. When feelings present themselves, do not judge them—they may be quite unique, but they are your heart and mind's message to you. Instead, acknowledge your emotions by identifying or labeling them (for example, *I feel scared* or *I feel tired*). Sometimes talking with a supportive friend can not only help validate your feelings but also ensure you are not left alone with intense emotions. If you are overwhelmed, you can express yourself through drawing or exercise instead of talking or writing. Expanding how you express your grief can help you experience it in new and perhaps more helpful ways.

For some people, actively engaging their grief may feel counterintuitive; that is, they may feel more comfortable avoiding it. If this describes you, be assured: The emotional pain you are feeling will actually become less intense the more you acknowledge it. By not discussing it, you are giving the painful feelings more power over you. For long-term success, it is best to make the choice to experience your grief now.

As you grieve and begin to heal, do not feel pressured to "get over" your grief. I recall Jason, whose wife got angry with him when she felt he had grieved long enough after his father died. She kept telling him to "get over it," and instead, he listened to his feelings. No matter what anyone says, allow yourself the time to think about your loss, the freedom to heal, and the right to take care of yourself by giving—or even asking others for— what your mind and body might need.

I've provided you with prompts to complete to begin journaling. (For more prompts, see page 97). Try to label or describe feelings (for example, *I feel saturated, weighed down,* or *frightened*). If you are having trouble putting your words to paper, you can set a timer for a few minutes and just write without judging, hesitating, or lifting your hand from the paper.

WHEN I THINK ABOUT MY LOSS, I FEEL . . .

Numb. I don't want to engage
with it. It feels like too much
to deal with.
I feel upset and sad. And
angry that he did something so
incredibly selfish
I feel like it ruined my life
and my relationship wit my mother
and now I don't know where to go

Just Breathe

In stressful times, it's common to hear people say "Just breathe!"
Breathing is, of course, essential to our existence, but it's not something we particularly think about. Breathing is actually a profoundly
useful stress-reducing technique. Conscious breathing can teach
the nervous system to shift from a state of "fight-or-flight" to one of
"rest and digest." When we are stressed and upset, our bodies acti-
vate the fight-or-flight response. This is an unhealthy way to operate
for prolonged periods because our heart rates and blood pressure
rise while other systems, such as the digestive system, actually shut
down to conserve energy. Follow the instructions below to practice
breathing techniques to reduce your stress.

1. **Find a quiet place.** Sit in a comfortable position or lie down
   and close your eyes.

2. **Take a long, deep breath.** Breathe in through your nose,
   expanding your diaphragm, and then slowly release the air
   out of your mouth. Keep your breaths even and slow. If you
   are expanding your chest, you are not taking a good breath.
   To breathe into your diaphragm, lie on a flat surface with your
   hands on your abdomen so you can see and feel your diaphragm rising and falling.

3. **Let go of any thoughts that enter your mind.** They can wait.
   Simply focus on the pattern of your breath.

4. **For five minutes, just breathe.** At first, just breathing for even
   two minutes may seem like an eternity, but as you practice,
   and your mind is able to shift gears, you will find the time
   passes more easily and you become more relaxed. →

If you have any difficulty calming your mind to focus on breathing, you may find sitting in nature an easier way to decompress. You could also use music, a sound machine, or a flickering candle flame to focus your attention. If you continue to find it tough to sit quietly and breathe, try a progressive muscle relaxation technique. You will still focus on your breathing, with eyes closed, but while sitting upright in a chair. Concentrating on one muscle group at a time, starting with your feet and moving upward through all your muscles, contract each muscle group for five seconds and then release the contraction, imagining all the tension melting away onto the floor. This can help you recognize your areas of stress, and it feels great.

Every Experience Is Unique

I can't tell you the number of times people have asked me if something they are thinking or feeling is "normal." There is no absolute normal; the definition of normal is a personal one and is constantly changing depending on the situation. If you are concerned about whether something is normal, ask yourself if you are okay with the thought or feeling—and trust in yourself. The only caveat is that your thoughts and feelings should not push you to harm yourself or negatively affect your life.

Every experience of loss is completely unique, and unfortunately, even if you have been through losses before in your life, you may find yourself in uncharted territory, grieving very differently this time around. This is because this particular loss is different from other losses, and you have become a different person. The circumstances surrounding the loss, such as a sudden death compared with an expected one, can change how you feel about it. The age of the person who died, and your own age at the time, can likewise create a more significant impact. Your relationship with the

Robert's Story

When his best friend of 20 years died after a long battle with cancer, Robert found himself afraid he would never have that kind of relationship again. He would watch a movie and an inside joke would present itself, but he had no one to share it with—no one else would understand. There would never be the casual drop-over for a late-night beer, or the sharing of new milestones. He had other relationships in his life, but this lost relationship left a void.

When we experience a loss, we are grieving not just the loss of the physical person, but also the loss of who we were when we were with that person as well as the loss of the emotional investment we made in that relationship. Many people believe that when a death occurs, the relationship is gone. But you still have the memories of the person, so the relationship will continue, albeit one-sided. Your relationship with the person needs time to heal so that your raw emotions can scar over, so to speak, and you can begin to reflect on memories with increased pleasure instead of sadness.

person at the time of the loss—whether you have regrets, resentment, or other looming feelings—can change your experience. Try not to force yourself to feel or grieve in any particular way. Allow your experience of grief to be just as unique as you are.

How Grief Can Affect the Body

When our mind is working incredibly hard to make sense of a loss, it is common to become forgetful, unfocused, or preoccupied. There is a mind-body connection, and when our mind is full of stress, the body will react (see "Just Breathe," page 15, for more on how the body reacts to stress). When people are experiencing a loss, they may also develop various physical symptoms, either due to the stress of the grief or because they are avoiding their feelings. These physical symptoms are your body's way of demanding you take care of yourself, and they should not be ignored. Some people experience digestive problems, stomach pains, or changes in appetite. Others might complain of sleep changes due to nightmares, racing thoughts, hypervigilance, or sadness. Some people may experience headaches, anxiety, or muscular pains, while others find relationships difficult to maintain. Over time, if you work through your grief, these symptoms will almost certainly diminish. If your grief is left unaddressed, however, the symptoms can become more serious and even snowball into additional physical issues.

If your grief is left unaddressed, the symptoms can become more serious.

When certain symptoms become severe, they should be addressed by a doctor or grief counselor. Grief that causes a sense of melancholy or depression for six months or more may be a sign of deeper and more critical distress (see page 59 for more about recognizing depression). Some people may experience complicated grief, in which the grief symptoms impair their ability to function and cause problems to compound. Sometimes after a loss, a person might begin to develop unexplainable medical ailments or symptoms similar to those experienced by the person who died; these are called psychosomatic symptoms and can feel very real. In these circumstances, it is imperative that you seek professional help to assist you in navigating your grief.

Think about how your body is feeling right now. Have you been sleeping? Have you taken the time to breathe? Have you noticed any changes in your body? Is there anything you should see your doctor about?

TODAY MY BODY FEELS...

Tired, in pain, stressed, overwhelmed.
I feel like my pain is better but today I just feel like going to bed and sleeping all day.

Misconceptions about Grief

Misconceptions about grief develop based upon our own or someone else's past experiences of grief. These beliefs may tell us how we should feel and act, dictate when we are allowed to grieve, or prescribe what to do to stop grieving. Unfortunately, these misconceptions can lead us to believe that there is only one right way to grieve and cause us to feel inadequate or abnormal, and this can impair our healing. Grieving in your own way is the only right way to grieve. These are some of the common misconceptions I hear:

You should be over your grief by now. This misconception may also include the belief that once you have reached acceptance, you are done grieving, or that grief ends six months to a year after the loss. I remember Carla, who lost her husband to suicide and whose mother offered a prescription on how she should handle the death of her husband. She should grieve for six months by sitting alone at home, not working, and not going out with friends. After the six months, she could stop grieving, date, and remarry. However, this did not align with how she was feeling nor did it help her grieve her husband. Grief is not time-limited; it does not necessarily end. It may become less intense, but as long as you remember the person, you will still, on some level, grieve the loss. Triggers may continue to affect you throughout your life: certain places, songs, movies, or holidays may respark your sense of grief. Often even you will be surprised when such feelings resurface. The ideal journey of grieving involves learning to live with and grow from the loss, not to stop grieving.

You can't get over your grief because you are holding onto sentimental objects. Eradicating all the mementos you have from a relationship will not erase the relationship from your memories. More than likely, destroying these memories will cause you regret in the future. Deciding which mementos to save is part of your healing, and you should not feel pressured to put away or get rid of pictures or other mementos. They can be helpful in your grieving, serving as transitional objects between life before the loss and life after the loss..

You are supposed to follow the stages of grief. There are no linear stages that are supposed to be followed when experiencing a loss. Grief is more accurately described as a roller coaster of emotions. Often people reference the commonly known stages outlined by Elisabeth Kübler-Ross in her book *On Death and Dying,* but there is not just one way to experience grief. Trying to fit yourself into a specific stage will not help you heal. Be attuned to what you need and allow yourself to grieve in your own way.

Grief happens only after someone has died. Grief can happen after any loss—miscarriage, divorce, the death of a pet, even the loss of a home to fire or foreclosure—as well as in anticipation of a loss. Grief is also experienced due to secondary losses, such the loss of other relationships upon death of a mutual friend. This type of misconception makes the judgment that you're not actually grieving and your feelings are wrong. But feelings are never wrong.

You are better off grieving alone. No one should have to grieve alone. Sometimes people feel like withdrawing into a cocoon until they have resolved their own feelings, but part of grieving is having your grief understood and accepted by others. There are times for solitude and reflection in your grieving, and this can be helpful, but it is also important to maintain relationships and a support system throughout your grief.

Feeling a certain way after a loss makes you a bad person. After a loss, we encounter a myriad of feelings and thoughts—such as guilt, anger, or shame—many of which do not seem rational or make sense. We usually limit the expression of our feelings to what we think is normal or acceptable. However, no feeling or thought that you are having makes you a bad person. These thoughts, even the seemingly irrational ones, just make you human. As you start to share what's going on inside you with others, you will undoubtedly find that you are not the only person who has these thoughts and feelings.

Society's View of Grief

Over the past century, death has been removed from the home and placed in hospitals, nursing homes, and funeral homes, away from family and friends. It was shifted into our peripheral view so we would not have to see it. This wasn't a sudden change, but gradually over time we have moved away from a face-to-face understanding of life and death. Perhaps with the increased benefits of medicine, in which death is delayed for longer periods of time, we have become less prone to witnessing death. Or perhaps as relocation becomes more prevalent and families spread out, the collective rituals of death have also diminished. People may come into town a day or two beforehand, attend funeral arrangements and services, then return to their lives, miles away, within the week.

Children have also become more sheltered from witnessing death. Whereas they once would have been a part of the process, seeing friends and family dying of illnesses or being part of the town processional, many children are no longer allowed to participate in funeral services because adults believe they are too young to understand. This can even apply to discussing the death of a family pet. For example, children might be told, "Dogs don't die, they go to live on a farm." So we now have a society where, though dying and death occur every day in our lives and on the news, it is something that happens outside of our own and our family's everyday reality.

As a result, we have generations of people who do not know how to face, handle, or talk about grief and tend to be uncomfortable with outward expressions of grieving. We sometimes feel ashamed or weak if we show our innermost emotions, so we don't allow them to be seen. As a society, we've come to see depression as something that must be avoided or hidden, and have ended up stigmatizing sadness instead of embracing and addressing it. Society has even established time limits on the length of time we should grieve, and "norms" limit us to grieving only particular relationships. After this brief period of time, we are expected to return to our life as if nothing has happened. When people do genuinely and openly express their feelings, we become uncomfortable and immediately look for the instantaneous fix, or worse, we might label the person as dramatic, needy, or even crazy.

This combination of societal issues can make it difficult for some to identify the need for help and to seek out support, but as we continue to look at grief as a normal healthy response, we will pave the way toward expressing ourselves more honestly and recognizing when we, or others, can benefit from help.

Handling Others during Your Grief

Cultural anthropologist Margaret Mead has been quoted as saying, "When a person is born we rejoice, and when they're married we jubilate, but when they die we try to pretend nothing has happened." People often do not know how to act around those who are grieving. Should they discuss the loss? Should they act as if nothing happened? It is a difficult situation for both the person experiencing the loss and their friends, family, and acquaintances. It might be easier to be around a grieving person who holds back their emotions, but there is very little benefit to this emotional self-control except making everyone around you comfortable. Your job while grieving is not to be thinking about how to make everyone else more comfortable with your feelings. Unfortunately, in addition to your own grief, you will have to manage other people's sometimes unpredictable and even hurtful reactions to the loss and to you.

The way people respond to your grief has very little to do with you and what you are going through; they are just reacting to their own feelings. Grief naturally leads to social discomfort. Some people will be silent and not say anything. Others will say something that upsets you. Friends and family may withdraw from someone who is grieving, "giving them their space," but consequently leaving the person to feel isolated and unsupported. Do not be shocked if some of your friends and family pull away. Some people do this because they think it is what you want, but they also might do this in an effort to heal themselves or protect their own emotions.

Your Rights in Grieving

While every relationship is different, and our ways of dealing with loss are varied, one thing that is universal is our litany of rights as a grieving person. Everyone has a right to be able to grieve in their own way and be supported in their grief. You should remind yourself of these rights when you are feeling pressured to respond or feel a certain way during your grieving process.

A Griever's Rights

- I have the right to grieve in my own way and at my own pace.

- I have the right to grieve differently than anyone else because my experience is different than anyone else's experience.

- I have the right to not live up to my own or someone else's expectations about how I should grieve.

- I have the right to feel and express all of my feelings as they happen, even if they do not make sense at the time.

- I have the right to trust myself, my thoughts, and my feelings.

- I have the right to openly talk about my grief even if it makes others uncomfortable.

- I have a right to set limitations, maintain my own boundaries, and say "no."

- I have a right to actively pursue people, places, and situations that will help me.

- I have a right to sever relationships with those who are not supportive or who make me feel inadequate or inferior.

- I have a right to pursue spiritual and emotional growth.

- I have a right to engage in spiritual and cultural practices.

- I have a right to make changes in my life.
- I have the right to choose my priorities.
- I have the right to make mistakes.
- I have the right to change my mind and then change my mind again.
- I have the right to have good days and bad days.
- I have a right to experience joy and have fun in my life.
- I have the right to remember the person and celebrate their life.
- I have a right to grieve for as long as I need to.

We often respond to someone who is grieving how we think we would want others to respond to us. Some of the comments people will say may be based in religious beliefs, such as "It's God's will" or "part of God's plan," "Everything happens for a reason," "They are in a better place," or "Now you have an angel in heaven."

Other people might try to intellectualize the loss with statements such as "He lived a full life," "It could have been worse," "We all have to die someday," "They would want you to get on with your life," "Time heals all wounds," "What doesn't kill you makes you stronger," or "Perhaps it is better this way."

Some people will try to distract you from your grief. "You have to move on because you have others to take care of," "Be thankful for all that you have," or "Be brave for the children."

Even simple attempts to relate to you while you are grieving, such as "I know how you feel," can be downright insulting. These sayings can all hurt because they minimize your loss and can cause you to feel isolated and alone in your grief.

How can you handle these types of statements? Well, first try to keep in mind that most people are just trying to be supportive in their own way, however awkward or poorly chosen their words can be. I remember Stella, who lost her husband, said, "I learned never to hold anything said at a funeral against somebody." There's grace and truth in this—people don't know what to say, and often in a desperate attempt to come up with a comforting response, their words come out wrong. There is no benefit in lashing out at someone who is attempting to be supportive—it will probably just cause you to feel regret. And if somebody is trying to cause conflict, the best thing you can do for yourself is walk away, without a word. If someone makes a statement you feel you must respond to, you can say, "That's just not what I need to hear right now," or "Thanks, but I need time to feel that way about it." Or, instead of responding at all, you could ask for what you do need. People feel awkward when they don't know what to do, so give them something to do. Tell them you need someone to vent to without any judgment or solutions, or someone to go out with once a week. And if you don't have a clue what will feel right, tell them that: "I don't know what I need, but I will let you know if something's not working for me." People are often paralyzed at the moment they are needed because they are afraid to say or do the wrong thing. So guide them.

Most people are just trying to be supportive in their own way, however awkward or poorly chosen their words can be.

In addition to face-to-face interactions, people also connect through social media. Because grief is such a personal experience, you might be unsure about using this medium and friends and family might also be confused about utilizing social media to communicate with you.

Above all, do what is comfortable for you. If posting about your loss feels natural and cathartic, it can be a good way for others to send their

Ann's Story

Ann was grieving after losing her daughter to leukemia. Several weeks after her daughter died, she went shopping, and as she was entering the store, she saw a woman she knew out of the corner of her eye. Ann had not seen this woman since her daughter died, and the woman was obviously terrified of running into Ann, because she scurried and hid behind a pole outside the store. Stunned (and a little amused) by this reaction, Ann reported what she witnessed to her family. She and her family would go on to use that analogy for years—"hiding behind a pole" became the go-to phrase to describe anyone who avoids or is afraid to approach someone simply because they don't know what to say.

Although friends and family may want to be supportive, they may become intimidated and avoid you when they are faced with trying to say or do the right things. Don't take it personally. When people do not know how to manage their own feelings of grief, it can be impossible for them to understand how to be supportive of yours.

condolences and provide support. You might also find it convenient in relaying information to extended family and friends. However, if you have not gone public with your loss and begin to receive condolences over social media, you might feel violated. A simple response such as, "Thank you for your support. At this time I would like to spend time with my family and will post information when I am ready," can set expectations for interaction. Just remember that you can control how you use social media and that written exchanges can be misinterpreted. If you find yourself confused by a comment or find it inappropriate, staying off social media and relying on in-person conversations will likely be more beneficial for you.

Coping through Self-Care

Grief is emotionally and physically draining, so it is important to take care of yourself. Self-care, including a well-balanced diet, plenty of rest, exercise, and relaxation, are the best gifts you can give yourself in trying times. Self-care means taking care of your own needs, and may be as simple as carving out time to take a long hot bath, going for a run, or making the time for friends. All of these things help you to cope, reduce your stress, and allow you to heal. Before you can take care of work, family, finances, or anything else in life, you should take care of the most important person in your world: you. As you take care of your own needs, you will find it easier to manage other things demanding your attention.

Focus on Yourself

In the fast-paced world we live in, we rarely take the time to sit with our thoughts and feelings and just think. We are action oriented: *I must do something about the event to fix it and move on.* Stop and think about what you need right now. You are the most important person in your life, and if you aren't accustomed to regarding yourself in this manner, this is the time to make yourself the top priority. Many times when we consider doing things for ourselves, we feel guilty or pressured to take care of others instead. Do not feel guilty about taking care of yourself. Don't view it as self-indulgence or shame yourself. You *are* important, and if you care for your own needs, you can better tend to those of others. Start by making a list of what you need and want. Maybe you need to reconnect with people or maybe you just need to treat yourself to fishing, painting, or taking a class. This is your chance to have no-guilt "me time." Take some time to connect with your own feelings, wants, and needs—this is all part of the healing process. At the very least, it's a positive distraction, and at best, it can help kindle or renew passions and energies that you may not have felt in a long time.

Although taking care of your own needs may lead you to consider making major life changes, immediately after a loss is not the best time to do so. For example, this is not the time to become vegan, begin a strenuous workout regimen, or move to the other side of the country. Impulsive lifestyle changes can add to your stress and can be detrimental to your long-term well-being. It is generally recommended to wait about a year before you make these types of decisions. For now, focus on taking care of your body, mind, and spirit.

Restorative Behaviors

After a loss, it can feel like a part of yourself is missing. What can you do to start to feel whole again? The positive actions you take to bring equilibrium back into your life are what we call restorative behaviors. Important restorative behaviors include being active in your grief by engaging your emotions, listening to your body, and meeting your own needs. What works for one person might not work for another, so do not get discouraged; keep pursuing new ways to find balance in your life.

RELEASING EMOTIONS

You lost someone important in your life. You are going to have feelings about this, so let them out in every way. Talk about them to friends, write in your journal, paint a picture of them, do anything you can to get those thoughts and feelings out in the open. When you let your emotions out, you will likely feel a release, like a weight being lifted off your shoulders. This is real—you have released some of your burden. Most people do not realize the importance of having their words heard by someone else. By sharing, you decrease the isolation of feeling like such a thing only happened to you, and can perhaps even help others find the words to express their own grief with you.

SLOWING DOWN

During times of grief, it is normal for some people to experience cognitive disorientation, or an inability to think clearly. This is a message from your body telling you it needs you to slow down. Ruminating is common with grief because you are trying like crazy to resolve or make sense of the loss, all the while losing your ability to think about other things. Even if it feels like you're unable to concentrate, your brain is actually concentrating intensely, just on something else. The solution to this is to do things you find relaxing, like sitting on a beach, getting a massage, listening to music, going on a hike, or playing golf. And give yourself permission to *not* finish everything on your to-do list each day. By taking some time to relax your overworked mind, you will find it much easier to focus.

EATING WELL

During times of emotional discomfort, we have a tendency to gravitate toward unhealthy comfort foods. Do not banish these foods completely— they are comforting for a reason—but do consume them in moderation, as it is important to eat a healthy, balanced diet and care for your body. Although this is not the time to try a challenging diet, it is critical to maintain healthy eating habits. Make sure to eat foods from all of the food groups, including lots of fruits and vegetables, grains, proteins, and dairy, and make sure to drink plenty of fluids to keep hydrated and flush away toxins. Many whole foods (that is, not processed foods) are filled with antioxidants and energizing, immune-boosting nutrients that can make a huge difference in how you feel. Try to limit pre-packaged processed foods and fast food. Although convenient, these fat-laden foods leave you too full for healthy foods, and their excessive salt and other additives lend to bloating, high blood pressure, and other maladies. Cooking meals at home, having healthy meals delivered, or asking a friend to cook can be a better alternative, and this is a great way to feel comforted. If you lose your appetite, remember you still need to take care of your body, so do not skip meals. Keeping simple, whole snacks like nuts, fresh produce, and cheese on hand can make it easy to just reach out and grab something that will satiate you and keep your energy up when you're feeling low. If you don't feel like you are getting enough vitamins in your diet, taking a daily multi-vitamin can help ensure some balance.

EXERCISING

Exercise helps your brain think more clearly, stabilizes your feelings, and improves your health. Try to exercise a little every day. Granted, it may be the last thing you feel like doing right now, so start small. It is better to start an exercise regimen with realistic expectations so you have the best chance of feeling successful. If you don't already have one, start with simple exercises that you can incorporate in your normal routines, like going for a short walk during your lunch, using the stairs instead of the elevator, or starting each day with some stretches. You might decide you need a class to keep you motivated to exercise, so consider joining a spin, yoga, dance, or kickboxing class. Yoga might be a good choice if your energy is low, while kickboxing can provide a release for feelings of frustration or anger. If you enjoy independent exercise, try swimming, walking, running, or biking. Being outdoors is doubly beneficial, because you soak up the sun's ultraviolet rays (even in winter) that provide mood-boosting vitamin D. All in all, the type of exercise is not nearly as important as finding something you enjoy and will consistently do.

Do you realize how strong you are? You probably have had changes through-out your life—like moving to a new school or ending a long relationship—and you managed to get through it. What did you do to navigate your emotions in the past? Who were the people that supported you? How did those events change you, and how did they make you stronger? Consider the things you do in life that make you feel empowered, confident, or successful. Instead of identifying the things you want to improve about yourself, focus on cultivating the strengths you already have. Take some time to write about past losses or major changes and what you did to cope. You may look at this list and say to yourself, *I forgot about that. I thought I'd never get past that!* Using your past experiences as a guide can be helpful in developing a sense of clarity and a realization of the life challenges you have already gotten through, as well as some direction on how to become stronger once again.

SOME MAJOR CHANGES AND PAST LOSSES WERE . . .

- moving around all the time as a child
- getting ill in college
- getting ill in England
- losing my job
- not knowing what to do now

I OVERCAME THOSE CHALLENGES WITH MY STRENGTHS BY . . .

- still working at it...
- Persistence

SURROUNDING YOURSELF WITH SUPPORTIVE FRIENDS

One mistake people make when they are grieving is believing that they are alone. Reach out to your friends, family, and neighbors. Often people want to help in times of grief but do not know how. Include people in your grief: ask them to go out to dinner with you, encourage them to check in on you, or even just have them sit and watch television with you. Human contact is essential to our well-being, so even if you have to force yourself a bit, surround yourself with those who can support you. Although it is completely normal to want to spend time alone while you are grieving, and important to spend time in quiet reflection, time alone should be balanced with time with others.

LAUGHING

Often people feel that if they are not sad about the loss, it makes them a bad person. You do not have to express your grief every moment of the day to be grieving. Life needs balance, so for all the sad feelings you are experiencing, it is important to spend just as much energy smiling and laughing. Although it may feel awkward to make yourself laugh, a few good belly laughs can change your entire outlook on your day. Try to act silly, sing lighthearted songs, or watch a funny movie. Seek out a friend who knows how to make you laugh. Do whatever it takes to get some laughter in your day. A good laugh is truly medicine and can make even the worst days feel more bearable.

CELEBRATING YOUR LOVED ONE

There is no better way to honor a loss than to celebrate the person's life. You can celebrate the person's birthday with friends and family to retell stories and share memories, plant a tree in their memory, participate in their favorite activity, or do something they had always wanted to do but did not get the chance. This is a way of actively remembering the person, honoring your relationships with them, and celebrating their life. When the stories get rolling, you can almost feel that person's presence with you.

Sarah analogized that when her husband died suddenly, she dropped all the "strings." These "strings" were her responsibilities—like those of a puppeteer. She had to prioritize and choose to pick up the strings that were most important. The first strings she picked up were her parenting duties—she was left with five young children, so this could not wait. Friends and family helped. As time went on and her strength and resolve began to return, she picked up additional strings, returning to her volunteer work and other activities. Some strings, like a small fledgling business she had started with her late husband, stayed on the ground for good. But it was all in her power to take up or bypass, and she chose what worked for her in her "new normal."

Deciding what you need to find balance in your life may not come easily. Most restorative behaviors are asking you to simply take care of yourself and your own needs. If you have never made yourself a priority before, now is a great time to start.

Many people find celebrating their loved one through social media comforting. There are sites available to share condolences, create a memory page for people to contribute pictures or memories, or communicate the loss with people who might have not been informed. It is important to remember the audience when posting pictures or comments, as young children as well as older adults may be seeing the page.

You could also celebrate the person by keeping mementos. Some people may tell you that this does not let you heal, but on the contrary, seeing a photograph of that person can serve as a heartwarming reminder of the times you had together. Although it is important to keep some mementos, you do not need to save everything. Down the road, as you decide which mementos to keep, I suggest setting aside three boxes, one for things you

Meditation

Meditation is a widely utilized and successful stress reduction technique. It can help you focus, find clarity, be more rested, and make you feel more cohesive. Meditation has been shown to have health benefits beyond relaxation, such as decreasing the need for medication, lowering blood pressure, decreasing anxiety, and improving overall self-awareness. Several different types of meditation build on focused deep-breathing techniques (discussed on page 15). Read on for some common variations.

Guided Imagery   An exercise for your imagination, guided imagery means imagining yourself in a place that you find completely relaxing, free of physical or emotional concerns. While focusing on your deep breathing, picture yourself sitting on the beach of a tropical island staring off into the sunset as the waves lap along the shore; looking up at a star-filled sky on a warm summer night as the crickets chirp; or sitting near a warm wood-burning fire on a cold night as the logs crackle. Engage your five senses to imagine exactly what you would see, feel, smell, hear, and taste. Listening to a recording of nature sounds can help direct or enhance your imagination.

Mindfulness   This amazing tool simply involves focusing your attention on living in the present moment and being completely conscious of all that is around you. To prepare, silence your phone, since electronics are often the antithesis of mindfulness. Now slow down your thoughts and focus fully on your senses. While in guided imagery you are imagining your senses, with mindfulness you are acknowledging actual sensations. As you step into the shower, how does the water feel against your skin? Can you smell the soap? What does it sound like as the water runs to the drain? As you eat, chew more purposefully. How does the food feel in your mouth? What tastes can you sense? Being mindful means taking the time to notice the things around you and the things you do. This type of meditation can be done anywhere you are—your workplace, the grocery store, the park. It can help you be more present in your life, noticing things that might ordinarily go unnoticed and appreciating the depth and realness of the sights, sounds, and sensations of the world around you.

Movement Meditations   Tai chi and yoga are practices that engage your whole body in meditation. In addition to concentrating on your breath, movement meditations require physical activity and concentration on your muscles These meditations can be especially helpful if you find it difficult to calm your mind during sitting meditations. They are also a great way to introduce an exercise routine into your schedule. Classes or videos for movement meditations can be helpful for learning and practicing the techniques until you can do them on your own.

Daily Meditations   Inspirational written thoughts can help you change your current state of mind as you reflect on something abstract, greater than yourself, uplifting, or thought provoking. Many people read such daily meditations to search for deeper meaning in life. They can also help you gain a new perspective on your loss or even your life. Reading a meditation or prayer each morning can help set the tone for your day. Check the resources section for meditation and prayer websites.

want to keep or store, one for trash, and one for giving away—you are probably not the only person who would appreciate these mementos. Mementos tell stories, and giving them away is a special gift. Just make sure to keep some things for yourself. If you throw out everything in haste, you may regret the decision later.

MAKING LISTS

As you grieve, create to-do lists to help you stay on your life's course as you muddle through the turbulent moments. It is easy to become so focused on loss that life's obligations sit idle. People experiencing loss might drop the ball on their finances, neglect relationships, and allow life to become fragmented. Many people find that making lists of things that need to get done extremely helpful, especially when they are finding it difficult to concentrate. When you have a concrete list, it is easier to ask for help, and it's also a great way to prioritize. There is nothing wrong with assigning tasks to trusted friends and family if you feel unable to manage them. You can try to commit to completing a few tasks on your list each day. Making plans and achieving goals can be a stabilizing force when life is not feeling very straightforward.

GETTING A GOOD NIGHT'S REST

Getting a good night's rest means sleeping at night in a bed for eight hours and also getting out of bed in the morning (even when you don't feel like it). If you are struggling with the getting-out-of-bed part, ask a friend for a wake-up call. If you continue to wake up in the morning and do not feel rested, simple changes can help: using all-white sheets, letting natural sunlight come in the windows in the morning instead of using shades, sitting by a light therapy lamp during the day, or showering at night before bed and again in the morning. Sometimes allowing yourself to grab a nap during the middle of the day can be just what you need.

If falling asleep seems to be a problem for you, simple routine changes might make a difference. Doing a short exercise before going to bed can help the body relax, and meditation can calm the mind. Turn off electronics (television, computer, tablet) an hour or so before bedtime. Establish a peaceful nightly routine so your body is ready to go to sleep. Take a shower, brush your teeth, and read something light in bed to signal to your body and brain that it is time to sleep. If you have trouble with racing thoughts, you might want to keep a journal (or use the one in this book) next to the bed to write down all the thoughts you are having, which you can review in the morning. Much like sharing your thoughts with another person, writing them down unloads them from your "mental file cabinet" and allows you to rest.

Setbacks and Solutions

During your grief, you will have to navigate many hurdles. You may find yourself stuck in certain roles that don't allow you to grieve. You may find yourself in conflict with how you are grieving and how you believe you should be reacting to your loss. You may even be engaging in some self-defeating behaviors that make it impossible to reconcile your loss. It is important to acknowledge when these setbacks are happening so you can actively make changes. Healing takes time, but you may be doing things that are not helpful and that prevent you from moving forward. If you are unable to make the changes you want for yourself and are feeling stuck, it may be the right time to ask for help. Some common stumbling blocks are discussed in this chapter.

Grief Roles

Many people find themselves repeatedly fulfilling the same roles when they go through different losses. Some of these roles include the caretaker who meets everyone else's needs, the rational one who does not exhibit feelings and instead mediates the situation, the emotional one who is overwhelmed and distraught and cannot be asked to do anything, or the organizer who plans every detail for the family and keeps everyone on schedule. If you can identify with this situation, you should understand that fulfilling certain roles can affect how you are able to grieve. Maintaining a role may not be what you need during this loss, but because it is the role expected of you by others, you may be doing it anyway. If you find yourself stuck in a role that is preventing you from getting your own needs met, talk to the other friends and family members who are grieving with you, so together you can try to change what is expected of you, delegate tasks to others, and get what you need.

Destructive Beliefs

Destructive beliefs tell us how to react in a situation, even when it is not what we might need. A person might believe they should not cry even while grieving, or that they should be crying all the time. Some people believe they should be feeling better already, or beat themselves up when they start to feel better with the belief that they must not have cared about the person. Other people might compare their own grief with someone else's reaction, judging it as good or bad. Some of these beliefs might be influenced by the things people are saying to you after the loss, sending you messages about how you should grieve. For example, Mika, who had lost her husband, was told by a family member during the wake that she should wear less makeup so that people would know she was sad. These types of beliefs are destructive because instead of helping you, they cause you to feel worse about yourself when you are not reacting in accordance with the beliefs. The truth is, whatever you are feeling or thinking during the loss is not just okay, it's important—these are your body's and your mind's messages to you. Journaling about these beliefs or discussing them with a friend can be an easy way to acknowledge that they are not helpful to you. Letting go of these beliefs will help you be less judgmental about yourself and will allow you to grieve in whatever ways you need to.

The roles we maintain and our expectations about grief can influence how we allow ourselves to grieve. What are some of the expectations you had about how you would grieve?

I THOUGHT GRIEF WOULD BE . . .

easier, over more quickly, progress in a more linear fashion be easier because he was such a difficult person

organizing everything, not dealing
w/ my emotions, feeling numb,
just trying to get on with
everyday life, not feeling comfortable
discussing it w/ people because
I don't like crying in front of them

Self-Defeating Behaviors

In our grief, we may unconsciously act in ways that cause us to become stuck and impede the healing process. Although these behaviors may initially help us manage the stress of the situation, in the long run they end up being counterproductive. The reason people usually turn to self-defeating behaviors is that they think it is the right thing to do, but ultimately they end up unable to grieve and feeling worse. To begin overcoming self-defeating behaviors, read through the ones on the following pages and pay close attention to those you may recognize in yourself. Journal about some of the reasons you might be resorting to such behavior and how it might be hindering your healing. Think about some small things you could do to change it. Simply leaving yourself a note on your bathroom mirror as a reminder to not try to be perfect or asking a friend to challenge you to ask for help can work toward changing self-defeating behaviors. We all have a pattern of how we handle stressful situations, and you may not be able transform this pattern overnight, but recognizing what you are doing and challenging yourself to change can put these behaviors on the sidelines.

AVOIDING OR MINIMIZING EMOTIONS

When people feel unsafe or uncomfortable expressing their feelings, it can cause them to minimize or completely avoid their emotions. A person who minimizes tells people that they're "doing fine," but in doing so, ends up convincing others that they do not need support. She might be afraid that others could not handle it if she told them what she's feeling, or she might be afraid that once she starts to express her feelings she might completely fall apart. Rather than express her feelings she might hide them, and as a result may experience increased stress, anxiety, and even depression. If this describes you, try not to judge your feelings. They are your body's way of telling you what affects you—so try to find a way to get them out. If you are not the type to express your emotions, you can start getting in touch with them by thinking about a specific one and identifying what events might cause you to feel that way. For example, you may identify that going out in large groups is upsetting you. If that is the case, perhaps you can start working through your emotions by talking to somebody in a comfortable one-on-one setting. For now, simply limit outings to more intimate engagements. Feelings are always okay unless they involve thoughts of hurting yourself or others. In which case, you should seek immediate professional help.

SCAPEGOATING

Scapegoating focuses on finding fault, but sometimes there is no fault. The scapegoat is sometimes not the cause, just someone who feels safe for you to blame. Initially, scapegoating can help you control your feelings about the loss by projecting them in another direction. For example, there isn't anything wrong with suing an incompetent doctor or drunk driver. But seeking justice in itself may not make you feel better if you are focusing your energy on this endeavor to avoid your grief. Ultimately it is important to identify the feelings you are projecting onto the scapegoat and decide where they belong. If you are experiencing anger or frustration toward the person who has died, try writing them a letter or talking to them as if they were here. Some people write out all the feelings they are having on small pieces of paper and use a holding space, like a piggy bank, to safely store them, pulling them out one at a time as they are ready to deal with them.

RATIONALIZING

This is the behavior of relentlessly searching for the reason "why" something happened. The person may even believe that the loss is a punishment for a lifestyle, or is unable to acknowledge that there is no rational reason for the loss. Maria, who had a miscarriage, believed losing her baby was punishment for her past behaviors. This type of thinking makes the assumption that we live in a just world, and that if we live perfectly then nothing bad will ever happen—which is not true. This rationalizing search can become all-consuming and keeps the person from dealing with the loss or even living their own life. The person may withdraw or become depressed or obsessive. If you identify with this behavior, seeking daily meditations or exploring your spirituality can be helpful in gaining a different perspective. Is there a reason you could be given that would make the loss okay? The answer is probably no, so all the rationalizing in the world will not help you heal. Focusing instead on gaining a greater awareness of spiritual wisdoms and philosophies may open your eyes to a different way of experiencing your loss.

PERFECTIONISM

Perfectionism stems from a belief that you need to be in control of your feelings and behaviors and must only respond in specific ways. You believe others rely on you to be the cornerstone and they would fall apart if you were not the stabilizing force. This behavior usually corresponds to the roles you hold within the family. You might spend all your time making others proud because you feel you have never accomplished enough. You might be living your life for the approval of others. The longer you maintain perfectionism, the more likely you are to fear rejection for being who you are or develop feelings of inferiority. Building your self-confidence can be key to truthfulness with yourself and others. As a start, try some new activities or hobbies outside of your comfort zone. Success with them may increase your ability to try new roles and take additional safe risks. Spend some time doing things that *you* enjoy to take care of yourself, instead of always being there for others.

PROBLEM SOLVING

Instead of allowing themselves to grieve, the problem solver is running around trying to solve everyone else's problems. For example, the problem solver tries to change laws or raise awareness about the recent loss instead of grieving. Someone with this self-defeating behavior might become hypervigilant about how a person died and develop unhealthy fears or phobias about engaging in similar activities. Behind this behavior is the fear that if the problem solver slows down, they will have to face the loss. So they just keep going. If you can identify with this behavior, try to slow down and focus on your needs instead of trying to fix things. Avoid situations that can increase your anxiety, and instead choose activities that improve your ability to relax, such as reading, meditation, sports, or gardening.

ISOLATION

Seeking solitude and claiming that "no one can understand me" are two ways a person uses isolation behaviors. This person ends up verbally pushing others away for any number of reasons. Unfortunately, if you push people away long enough, you will find yourself alone. Being alone after a loss is important to some degree so you can fully engage in the process of grieving. When you're grieving, you may feel disconnected from friends or family, even when they are reaching out to support you. This can be a paralyzing feeling if you stay isolated too long. Soon you may become hopeless, feeling like you have no control over the direction of your life and that nothing will get better. It is so important to reach out for help and surround yourself with a positive support system. You may need to schedule weekly appointments with friends to make sure you are not isolating yourself.

PUNISHING YOURSELF

Some people try to punish themselves after a loss due to feelings of guilt or regret (see chapter on guilt page 69). They may feel as if they are to blame for the loss, that they should have been the person who died instead, or that they could have prevented it. This person imposes unrealistic expectations on themselves about the amount of control they have in life. It is simply not healthy to feel this amount of pressure. This type of person may engage in self-harm or risk-taking behaviors. If you are feeling guilt or regret, simple acts of kindness such as volunteering or participating in a fundraiser can help you to feel less punitive toward yourself. Dog sitting for a friend can be doubly beneficial: As you take care of the pet, you are also receiving affection in return.

Jorge's Story

Jorge was 17 years old when the car he was driving crashed, ejecting his best friend from the passenger seat. Although both he and his friend had been reckless in testing the limits of the car's speed and agility, Jorge was left mostly unscathed while his friend died. As time went on, everyone thought Jorge was handling the death of his friend well. When he returned to school, he was maintaining his GPA, working part time, and completing his community service requirements. He lost his license, but he never complained about having to bum a ride, wait for his parents, or walk home from work. It wasn't until the weather got warmer that his parents noticed the self-inflicted scars on his arm.

Though for months he had maintained an image of normalcy, Jorge had been punishing himself for being behind the wheel. He felt that expressing his feelings was a way of forgiving himself, so he would not talk about them. Together we separated the events that led to his friend's death from the feelings he had been experiencing since the loss. Focusing just on his feelings about losing his friend and their relationship, he was able to write poetry describing the sadness of losing his best friend. Over time, Jorge was able to discuss his own feelings of responsibility and anger, but only once he'd had the space to grieve.

Sometimes when we utilize self-defeating behaviors, we need someone else to support us without judging or challenging what we are doing to manage our feelings. Seeking support is one of the best things you can do if you find yourself struggling with grief. When you are ready to tackle the self-defeating behaviors, those same people can be an honest reflection of your experience and can help you to see more clearly.

Engaging Your Triggers

Memories of your loss will be triggered in a variety of ways: a conversation, a familiar place, a phrase, a smell, a piece of music, a particular time of the year. People who experience these triggers try to plan their lives around them to avoid painful memories. The unfortunate reality is that you cannot avoid triggers. Even years later, people will find themselves suddenly overwhelmed by grief after experiencing a trigger. It does get easier, but your grief will always be with you, even in some small way. I encourage people to actively engage in things that trigger their grief. By engaging your triggers, you do not allow them to control you—you learn to control them. Go to your favorite restaurant, do things you enjoyed together, remember the things they liked to say, and listen to their favorite music. It is important to remember these details about the person. At first this may be hard, but by continuously engaging your triggers, you are dealing with your feelings and not allowing your loss to dictate your life.

Some triggers come in the form of events, like holidays. These annual occurrences can be a trigger for many of the losses we have experienced in our lives. The need for support during these times is immense, but you will get through it. There is nothing wrong with participating in the holiday and simply talking with those around you about how hard it is or what you miss. It's okay to cry! If while participating in the holidays, you realize it feels fake or you are just going through the motions, find ways to make it more enjoyable. If you need new traditions, creating them can be a powerful experience in its own right. The objective here is to not deliberately avoid situations, places, or people in your life. Engage your triggers and change them to fit your needs—whether that means stopping   →

in at an annual party instead of staying all night, exchanging checks to favorite charities instead of exchanging gifts, or learning to play that special song on the piano. Please be careful not to fall into isolation during the holidays, as this can compound your grief. Annual triggers will not go away, so come up with a plan on how you want to continue to celebrate these. And if it doesn't work, change it!

MEDICATIONS AND ALCOHOL

Although it is socially acceptable to enjoy the use of alcohol during the grief process, it is important to limit its use. This is also true for over-the-counter medications, prescription medications, and other mood-altering substances. Doctors will sometimes provide a prescription during times of grief to facilitate a sense of relief during the initial shock of the loss. A friend may share their prescriptions with you with the same intentions. Unfortunately, as thoughtful as this seems, prescription medications should only be utilized when prescribed by your doctor, never shared, and only taken according to the prescription label. Abuse of medications or alcohol not only decreases your ability to grieve, it can also lead to health, financial, social, or legal problems. If you find that you need alcohol or a drug to get through your day, please speak to a health-care professional.

Seeking Help

After a loss, there are often initially swarms of people who surround you and support you throughout the farewell rituals. Then everyone goes back to their lives and you may be left feeling unsupported and alone. There is no reason you should ever have to go on this journey alone. You may have a support system of friends and family, but there are also many support groups that can provide comfort, camaraderie, and understanding, and counselors who can help support you in this transition.

Within your personal social circle, you may have friends and family members who you talk to about your problems, and initially these might be the first people you turn to for support. Unfortunately, these may not always be the right people to talk about your loss. Some people feel uncomfortable talking about grief, and it may take a few tries to find the right friend with which to make this connection. Be sure to choose friends or family members who can be supportive, nonjudgmental, and caring, and realize that other friends may be supportive in different ways.

Support groups can provide comfort, camaraderie, and understanding.

When someone is struggling with grief, I almost always refer them to a support group. Support groups facilitated by a trained professional are extremely helpful, because they can help us put words to feelings that we cannot easily express, and they also challenge our misperceptions about grief, which is easier in a group setting. Being around people who have recently experienced a loss can also provide a sense of relief. If you are looking for a support group for grief, contact your local hospice organization or house of worship and ask for a referral for your specific situation.

Although social networking might seem like a great way to find people to discuss your loss, I strongly discourage online support groups. Social networking can be a great tool for social issues, as you can reach out to people with similar experiences and find a support system. Unfortunately, many of these groups are not facilitated by a grief counselor and are left unmonitored. There might be some that are worthwhile, but there is no way to know the motivations of the other participants in the group. These types of groups can cause more harm than good. Discussions about your grief should take place face-to-face in a supportive environment.

If you decide you want the support of a mental health professional, there are many different types of counselors who can help. Grief counselors can guide you on your journey through grief; a spiritual counselor can help you explore your faith; behavioral therapists can help you change self-defeating behaviors; and a life coach can help you with goal setting. If you are struggling with any aspect of your grief, whether it is feeling stuck in a pattern of negative thinking, thinking your grief is abnormal, or simply seeking someone trained to talk about these kinds of issues, there is no better time to ask for help. It is especially important to seek the guidance of a professional if you are using alcohol, drugs, or medications to manage your grief, if you notice a decrease in your overall health or appearance, or if you are unable to work or take care of your family or yourself. You might begin seeing a therapist only to find that you and the therapist are not a good match. Don't give up. There are many different types of counselors who can meet your personal style and therapeutic goals. If you are not happy, ask for a referral. Ask around—people are usually glad to share this information. The right counselor for you is out there.

How often and how long you see the counselor will depend on your goals. Short-term intervention-based therapy can be utilized over the course of a few months, while psychoanalytic therapy can be explored for years. Talk with your counselor about your expectations.

Emotions and Reactions

Loss is a time of emotional chaos. Feelings do not come at convenient times or on a schedule; they can be intrusive, disruptive, and demanding of your attention. They can come barreling out of nowhere and leave you feeling exposed. Grieving is a time to turn inward to embrace all of your feelings. This is not the time to interpret or judge them. Allow yourself to feel because all of your emotions are normal—they are your body's messages to you. Throughout this section of the book, we will discuss some common feelings and reactions to grief, including sadness, anger, guilt, anxiety, disbelief, and shame. We will consider some causes of these feelings, how others might react to them, and methods for coping.

Sadness

"Grief is like the ocean; it comes in waves ebbing and flowing. Sometimes the water is calm, and sometimes it is overwhelming. All we can do is learn to swim." —Vicki Harrison

Sadness is a natural reaction that you may have for weeks, months, or years after a loss. You have lost someone you cared about, the relationship that you had with the person is forever changed, and the future you had envisioned is altered. Sadness is generally the easiest to express after a loss because it goes along with what others expect you to feel. Although it is the commonly expected reaction, many people presume that after a short period of time, sadness will go away. Sadness, however, is a broad term that encompasses many different feelings and reactions, and the causes of these feelings may continue for a long time even when you have reconciled with your loss.

After a loss, your mind and body need time to reorganize themselves. For a while, you might not be sure what to do, and that's okay. Sometimes you will have racing thoughts and insomnia. At other moments you won't be able to concentrate because you are simply unable to stop thinking about the loss. This can cause you to feel exhausted or unmotivated, reduce your interest or pleasure in activities, and even cause you to question your existence. There is a lot to think about, and you need time to figure it out. You may unconsciously begin to simplify your life by not eating, dismissing your personal hygiene, or neglecting your personal life. Although this may appear to others as just "being lazy," grief can be truly exhausting and you are just spending your limited energy in a different way.

Feelings of loneliness can appear because that person left a void in your life. Without that person, you may have lost your own identity as a friend, partner, child, or caregiver. It's common to isolate yourself from others because you believe no one can understand the relationship you had, and that you will never have another relationship like the one you lost. You might recognize the need to fill the void left in their wake but then worry you are not honoring the person by doing so.

As more and more feelings about the loss come out, you might be drained, emotionally exhausted, or think there is nothing left to give. To protect yourself from intense grief, your body might limit your ability to feel, causing you to be emotionally numb. If you are overwhelmed, the remedy is not to suppress emotions, but rather to give in to them. Your body will need a release such as crying, even uncontrollably at times.

Maybe you see the person in your dreams or think you see him or her in familiar places. Some people look for signs from the person, such as hearing a song when they are having a bad day or finding something that belonged to the person on an anniversary. These experiences hold special meaning and come from an overwhelming sense of missing the person. Those signs existed when the person was still alive, they just have greater significance now. It's an interesting phenomenon when we stumble across a sign of that person, especially at certain times. Those signs reflect our heightened awareness of that person's impression on us and our continued connection with them once they are no longer a part of our daily lives.

What Does Sadness Look or Feel Like?

- Confusion or inability to concentrate
- Intrusive or racing thoughts
- Insomnia or increased desire to sleep
- Loss of energy and feeling tired
- Lack of motivation to do things or take care of yourself
- Reduced interest or pleasure in activities
- Change in appetite
- Loneliness
- Isolation or thinking that no one can understand what you are feeling
- Feeling empty, drained, or numb
- Crying, sobbing, and wailing
- Recurrent dreams about the person or loss
- Longing for the person or thinking you see the person

Coping with Sadness

Sadness expresses itself in different ways and can happen at different times after the loss. The initial shock can delay the reaction of sadness; conversely, triggers can continuously bring out these feelings for years. After the rituals of loss have ended and friends and family have gone back to their daily lives, the intense reactions of sadness might finally set in. The feelings may also become more intense as time passes before they become more manageable, because the realization of how the loss is going to affect you becomes greater once you are alone with your thoughts.

Suggested methods to manage sadness involve engaging in activities that allow you to gain equilibrium again. Balance sad feelings with happy feelings, alone time with social time, the inability to make decisions with making simple decisions. Do things that give you a sense of stability and comfort as your mind and body figure out how to manage the loss.

- Think/write about a memory that made you laugh/smile.
- Spend some time every day being sad. Give yourself permission to cry.
- Spend some time every day doing something you enjoy.
- Having people around can decrease your sense of isolation, so keep friends and family nearby. Spend some time alone, but balance this with social activities.
- Physical touch can be soothing when you feel lonely, so ask for a hug.
- Keep decisions simple when feeling unfocused.
- Maintain a peaceful nightly routine to maximize the likelihood of a good night's rest. Take naps if you need them.
- Cook or have someone prepare nourishing meals.
- Take care of personal hygiene daily. Shower and get dressed every day.
- Decide to get dressed up and go out.
- Find a grief group to talk with about your loss.
- Spend time in genuine prayer, voicing what you are grateful for and asking for comfort.

Until someone is gone, it is often difficult to know how we are going to be affected. Identify what struggles you are now facing after the loss.

THE HARDEST PART ABOUT LOSING YOU IS . . .

....

....

....

....

....

....

....

....

....

....

....

....

....

....

....

....

Clinical Depression

Although the word *depression* is commonplace in today's society for labeling feelings of sadness, it actually has a specific definition with clinical criteria and can only be diagnosed by a licensed clinician. It cannot be diagnosed by the Internet, your neighbor, or your family. The *Diagnostic and Statistical Manual of Mental Disorders (DSM)* does not classify grief itself as a disorder because it is a normal part of the human experience, but it does maintain that prolonged grief could lead to clinical depression. Clinical depression is a sadness that causes significant impairment in your ability to function in your social, personal, or work life. People who experience clinical depression often express that their grief feels like quicksand in which they are sinking, and, they cannot get out.

Although the actual diagnosis is of little importance to a person experiencing grief, people always want to know if they are "normal," which is understandable. The definition of "normal," however, is somewhat fluid. It depends on what you are currently experiencing, how long you have been experiencing it, and how it is impacting your life. Even though you might meet certain criteria (or not), the diagnosis is still subjective on your experience. It is best not to wait until you think you are clinically depressed to get help. If you feel stuck or unsupported in your grief, or just want to talk about your loss, or if someone suggests that you might need to talk to a professional about your thoughts or feelings, please speak to a counselor.

For a table outlining the differences between sadness and depression, see page 159.

Dealing with Others

As noted earlier, people have a tendency to feel uncomfortable with vulnerable feelings such as sadness, so when they see you vulnerable, they will want to do something to try to comfort you and take the sadness away. They might see you unable to concentrate and offer to help get things done around the house. They might sense your loneliness and listen and be supportive or try to get you out. They might also try to "fix it" and make suggestions about how you should be acting to get over your grief. And although virtually everyone cries at some point in their lives, and crying is a normal part of grief, crying may cause people to want to distract you or suggest you keep yourself busy. Although these measures are meant to be consoling, some things will not be. Listen to people's suggestions and mentally reject those that you do not find comforting. Let people know you appreciate their concern and ask for the help you need.

Anger

*"Anger is an acid that can do more harm to the
vessel in which it is stored than to anything on
which it is poured."* —Mark Twain

When people feel like they have no control in life, they tend to seek ways
to regain control. Losing someone can make you feel powerless, and
reacting with anger can make you feel, well, powerful! A person may
experience anger toward themselves, the doctors involved in the loss, a
higher power, or even the person who died for abandoning them. Anger
can be healthy as it can motivate you to keep going, but it can also become
destructive if it hurts you or your relationships.

When you experience too many feelings all at once, many times it
will come out as an intense, even explosive emotional outburst. Behind
that explosion might lurk feelings of pain, hate, blame, resentment, rage,
jealousy, confusion, and fear. Anger might very well be a projection of
the emotional pain you are feeling but are unable to express. Often it will
come out directed at the family and friends who are your most supportive
allies, and this can cause rifts in your relationships. When people feel
vulnerable, they gravitate toward expressing anger, which they believe
demonstrates their strength instead of their vulnerability. On the other
hand, while trying to hold in all the other emotions you are having, you

may become increasingly tense or agitated. When you are consumed with anger, little things might bother you and you may find yourself increasingly impatient, frustrated, and overwhelmed.

People try to understand why something had to happen, and can become resentful when life feels cruel or unfair. Feelings of anger over what you cannot control are normal. You might question why the loss happened. Why did it happen to you? Why couldn't you stop it? What did you do to deserve this? You might personalize the loss, and feel that the loss was unfair and you did not deserve it. In feeling unable to control life, some people might seek control in their own existence by engaging in risk-taking behaviors, self-injury, or active aggression, such as fighting.

Feelings of anger over what you cannot control are normal.

Anger often comes from a sense of wanting someone to blame. A person might dump all of their feelings onto someone else, feeling that person caused the loss or could have prevented it. Sometimes they even blame themselves, feeling they had some control over the outcome. They might blame the person who died because "they could have made better choices," or even a higher power for "allowing this to happen." Blaming others comes from wanting to find a reason for the loss.

Anger is a reactive expression of feelings that can provide a release and make other people aware that we need help. And ultimately, acknowledging the emotions that underlie this anger gives us the opportunity to explore our own beliefs about life and death, fairness, justice, personal responsibility, and our powerlessness.

What Does Anger Look or Feel Like?

- Intense, often explosive emotions
- Arguing with family and friends
- Tenseness or agitation
- Impatience
- Becoming easily frustrated or overwhelmed
- Resentment
- Questioning the reasons for the loss
- Personalization of the loss, feeling like you are a victim
- Risk-taking behaviors
- Self-injury
- Fighting
- Blaming others, yourself, the person, or a higher power for the loss

Coping with Anger

To cope effectively with an angry reaction, find healthy methods for releasing the anger. For some it might be better to employ relaxation techniques, while others might find a physically active approach more beneficial. Try to compartmentalize your anger—while letting it out is good, some places are better than others for this. Consider your "safe places" to express yourself and commit to using them exclusively.

Once you've established a foundation, map out strategies and activities that help you release this negative energy:

- Allow yourself to be angry and let it out.
- Talk about your anger with a supportive friend.
- Try stress-reducing techniques, muscle relaxation, and deep breathing exercises.
- Learn about yourself and your feelings by reading or listening to daily meditations.
- Engage in physical activities like bike riding, running, martial arts, boxing, or yoga, to release the emotional buildup.
- Scream in the open air, into a pillow, or to a willing friend.
- Pray for patience and peace.
- Use your energy in a positive way. Start a project, learn a hobby, or make something.

Dealing with Others

Initially, when we express anger after a loss, people understand our frustration, but over time, others' patience for our agitation will wear thin. Although anger does not cause people to run in the other direction like sadness does, our friends and family will only explain our feelings away for so long. If you express anger toward someone, there is a good chance they are going to express it right back at you, and your relationships will become impaired. People may become defensive, feeling that they are being attacked—which they are, even if your intention is not malicious. This can lead people to start avoiding you out of annoyance, while others may become afraid of you. It is important to apologize when you dump your feelings on others, blame them, or subject them to a tirade. If you are dealing with this issue, the key to coping is to find a way to release all of these excess feelings (consider some of the coping strategies above). Also, invite friends and family to remind you not to let it all build up.

Cathy's Story

Cathy was 15 years old when her father died in a car accident. She had seen a counselor briefly at the hospital, but had deemed the appointments unnecessary. She openly talked about her loss. She expressed that she was sad about the things he was going to miss out on, and how unfair it felt that that he was taken from her. Although she withdrew for the remainder of the semester until everything settled down, she returned to school in the fall as planned.

There was no way Cathy could understand all the ways she was going to miss her father until months after the loss. The anger's manifestation was a slow progression, building up as time passed and as events happened in her father's absence. She had played softball since she was little, and her father had always come to her games. After he died, she continued looking for him on the sidelines. He had been the person she went to when she had a problem. Her mother worked late, and her father had been the one home after school. But she was coming home to an empty house now.

Cathy became increasingly angry toward her mother. She had always been argumentative with her mother, and now that Cathy's father was gone, her mother expected some additional hostility. Since Cathy was a teenager, her mom decided this was normal. Cathy was angry that her dad died and left her, and the more time passed, the angrier she became. Why did this happen to her? Her destructive outbursts started when one afternoon she broke through the back door and window because she forgot her key. Throughout the year, her school friends stopped wanting to be around her as her moods and behaviors became increasingly unpredictable and destructive. $\rightarrow$

She began not coming home after school, staying out all night, and eventually she stopped adhering to any household rules. The anger built up until it exploded and she destroyed several cars on school property. Finally, her mother asked the court to mandate therapy.

Cathy was sent home with a journal in which to write every time she was angry at her mother, one that could be shared and discussed during therapy appointments. This became a lengthy list of things she blamed her mother for, but it became clear that mostly she missed her father and expected her mother to fill his role. It was an unrealistic expectation that, even with this insight, her mother could not fully meet. But her mother still wanted to be there for her. They joined the church choir, a mutual activity that allowed them to spend some time together each week. Cathy's aunt also got involved by having her over after school to help with her cousins' homework.

Anger does not want to be ignored, and if it is ignored it has a tendency to increase until it is acknowledged. It comes out, although often misdirected and unclear, and wants to be dealt with if you are willing. Allow yourself to be angry, but find positive ways to manage your anger.

Do you have feelings of anger or disappointment? Are you okay with these feelings? What are you going to do with these feelings? Take some time to explore your feelings of anger, disappointment, or frustration. But it is also useful to find balance, so consider feelings of gratitude as well. On the following page, use the prompt to think about some things you can be grateful for today.

I'M ANGRY THAT . . .

my brother was such a difficult person and my mother dealt with it so badly.

My life was so affected by his bullshit and continues to be.

I feel like there no where good for me to go now and everything is just so difficult.

I hate that he's idealized now. I'm so angry that he fucked up so much w/ everything.

my friends

having options in life

having a supportive mother

having Michael

being able to travel

having a good education

Guilt

"God grant me the serenity to accept the things I cannot change, the courage to change the things I can, and the wisdom to know the difference." —Reinhold Niebuhr, theologian-philosopher

After a loss, some people will blame others and become angry, while others will experience a profound sense of guilt. Guilt is a reaction to an internal conflict around how we believe we *should have* behaved versus how we *actually* behaved. Guilt is part of the human experience; we feel guilty when we do not meet someone's expectations, when we hurt someone else's feelings, or when we don't follow our own moral code. In a healthy sense, guilt shows us that we have empathy for others, we want to do what is right, and we are essentially good. Guilt after a loss comes out when we think we caused the loss or feel like we should have done something differently.

Guilt can happen when we have unfinished business with the person who has died. We might have regrets about the things we did or did not say or do, we might feel guilty about thoughts we had, or we might have made a promise that we did not get to keep. Some people might experience guilt over being relieved after someone who suffered for a long period dies. The thought of unfinished business can be a hurdle in reconciling our grief.

When we think about the loss, sometimes we start to focus on the actions we could have taken to change the situation. Persistent intrusive thoughts about what we could have done differently can become all-consuming. But the if-onlys, should'ves, would'ves, could'ves, and I-wish-I-hads, are useless expenditures of energy. There is no substantiation of the belief that we could have prevented the loss, yet we convince ourselves that we could have. Some people might begin to believe that they are solely to blame for the loss. Thinking you caused the loss is a huge responsibility, a burden that no one should carry, and can cause profound dysfunction, fear, anxiety, and insecurity.

Thinking you caused the loss is a huge responsibility, a burden that no one should carry.

At times, when we experience guilt we begin to punish ourselves. We may have self-critical thoughts, telling ourselves that we are worthless or inadequate. We feel we should not be enjoying life without the person, and condemn ourselves to living a life of misery. We might feel guilty for surviving or being uninjured, for saving ourselves, or for continuing to live. We might wonder why we are still alive, or even wish we had died instead.

Death can cause us to focus on the finality of life. We might be focusing on the importance of every interaction and relationship we have, and not want to leave the room or house, or end the day arguing with those we love. This can cause us to not express thoughts or feelings, and become excessively passive in interactions. But attempting to have perfect interactions and be a perfect person will only lead to more feelings of guilt and failure. Feeling that every interaction cannot be left without closure can cause a lot of stress. For some, realizing how short life is can also cause a sense of urgency to live life to the fullest, disregarding our own safety.

Although some guilt in our lives might be justified, the guilt we place on ourselves after a loss is unreasonable. It's easy to look back after an event and decide what should have happened; hindsight is great, but life does not work that way. All we can do is our best and not spend our energy regretting what we cannot change.

What Does Guilt Look or Feel Like?

- Regret
- Persistent intrusive thoughts
- Self-blame
- Fears, anxiety, insecurity
- Punishing yourself
- Increased self-critical thoughts
- Feeling worthless
- Avoiding enjoyment
- Focusing on the finality of life
- Becoming passive in interactions, avoiding conflict
- Attempting to be a perfect person

Guilt can arise from the sense that we should have done more or done things differently. Often people immediately rationalize their feelings of guilt away instead of simply acknowledging them. Take some time to think about your own feelings of guilt.

I'M OVERWHELMED BY GUILT. I FEEL GUILTY ABOUT . . .

....

....

....

....

....

....

....

....

....

....

....

....

....

....

....

....

WHY I SHOULDN'T FEEL THIS WAY . . .

....

....

....

....

....

....

....

....

....

....

....

....

....

....

....

....

....

....

....

....

....

Maggie's Story

Maggie's mother quietly died in her sleep after spending the greater part of a decade in a nursing home suffering from Alzheimer's disease. When she died, the family felt tremendous relief that her suffering was finally over. As life returned to normal after the funeral, there was a change in Maggie. She spent a lot of time journaling. She wrote about the life her mother had, how much she had sacrificed for her children, and how much of her own life she had missed due to the Alzheimer's. Maggie felt guilty about not visiting more often, even though she lived hours away with her own family and career. Maybe she could have found a nicer nursing home that her mother would have liked better. Surely there was more she could have done for the mother who gave her everything.

Maggie was so immersed in thinking about all the hardships her mother endured that she could not see all the wonderful things that had also happened. Her immense guilt hindered her from cherishing the moments she had with her mother. But as Maggie continued journaling, happy memories also arose: the story of her parents' first date, how her mother saved money to buy the house that would forever be known as "her house," and the tune she would hum every time one of her grandchildren cried in her lap. Over time, Maggie was able to let go of her guilt as the positive life experiences were remembered through her journaling.

Guilt can be a powerful emotion to manage because you can never know the answer to the "what if" questions. Life is often full of questioning if you have made the right choices and wondering what could have been. Our feelings of guilt can also give us the opportunity to embrace the finality of life and to be more present in our lives.

Coping with Guilt

Guilt can feel like a heavy weight that must be endured. After a loss, you may find yourself being more critical of yourself at just the time when you need to be more self-supporting. The key to overcoming guilt is realizing that it is self-imposed. Certainly someone can say something to make you feel guilty, but only you can allow yourself to feel guilty. Forgive yourself for not being perfect, for not making the right decisions, or for not saying the right things. As someone I know says of mistakes, "That's what happens when humans are involved!" This is a healthy viewpoint. None of us is perfect. Allow for regrets, forgive yourself, and make peace.

In the face of guilt, doing for others can provide solace and a needed boost of self-acceptance:

- Help someone else. You can volunteer or help a neighbor.

- Write a letter to the person you lost explaining why you feel guilty.

- Make a list of all the things you *don't* regret about your relationship. Were you a good friend? Did you make them laugh? Did you spend time together? Identify qualities about yourself that the person liked.

- Seek and/or pray for religious or spiritual forgiveness and peace.

- Talk to a trusted person. Often just talking about our guilt, saying it out loud, can help us realize our actual part in the loss.

- Assess your actual culpability. You might need to ask others what happened to get a clear picture.

- Finish unfinished business when you can, even if it no longer matters. If you are upset that you forgot to buy their favorite cereal, buy it and donate it. If you missed their birthday, celebrate it now.

- Practice forgiveness, for yourself and others.

- Recite the serenity prayer (see page 69).

Dealing with Others

Others looking in on your experience of guilt might feel you are acting illogically and try to convince you of that. Guilt is not logical, it is a
feeling, and feelings are not always rational or thought out—but they are
real. Some people might attempt to justify your actions by explaining to
you why you did what you did. You might have to tell them that you're
not seeking explanations or excuses, but instead just need to vent these
thoughts and feelings. Logically, we know we do not control these events,
but there may be a part of us that believes we could have. Just as you are
feeling responsible for the loss, many people are going to feel responsible for making you feel better. You do not need to be fixed, but you also
should not have to feel guilty for the rest of your life about something you
cannot change.

Anxiety

"Worrying doesn't take away tomorrow's troubles, it takes away today's peace." —Anonymous

Loss can remind us of our own mortality and bring our insecurities and fears to the surface. Most of the time we do not focus a great deal of attention thinking about life and death, but when someone dies, we may suddenly take stock of our lives. Sometimes this can help us identify changes we should make, like eating healthier or making sure to spend the holidays with family. Other times, this scrutiny can cause an unhealthy increase in anxiety.

If you begin to think about how the loss occurred, you might become anxious that the same thing could happen to you or someone else you care about. This can cause people to overreact and develop irrational fears. Fears are normal, they keep us safe and making good choices, but irrational fears can end up limiting our ability to live life. You might begin trying to control your environment by not allowing people you care about to drive, fly in planes, or travel far from home. You might become anxiety-ridden every time someone leaves the house or when you are alone. After any type of trauma, many people become hypervigilant, looking for problems everywhere in an attempt to avoid repeating the experience. Some people even develop paranoia or suspiciousness of other people in their

What Does Anxiety Look or Feel Like?

- Irrational fears
- Feeling fearful, cautious, or nervous all the time
- Hypervigilance
- Paranoia or suspicion of others
- Panic attacks
- Shortness of breath, feeling unable to breathe
- Nervous energy
- Feeling helpless to prevent crisis
- Recurring nightmares
- Inability to sleep
- Fear of being alone
- Obsessive behaviors
- Insecurity
- Feeling a need to make a change

lives. With this type of chronic anxiety, panic attacks can occur, leaving you unable to function in daily life. You might feel helpless in avoiding crisis. Anxiety can cause shortness of breath or nervous energy such as fidgeting or shaking your leg.

For some, nightmares or persistent thoughts about how the loss occurred may keep them awake at night. You might become afraid of the dark, afraid to be alone, or afraid to sleep. You might begin obsessively checking on family members throughout the night to ensure their safety.

Obsessive behaviors may develop from the constant effort to reassure yourself that you are okay, and can become disruptive to life.

Insecurity might arise when you realize that some of the roles the person had in your life might now have to be held by you. You might not feel competent to take over these responsibilities or have anxiety about facing a new situation.

Your anxiety may be causing you so much discomfort that you decide you need a big change to reduce it, like moving to a new home, changing jobs, or getting a new pet. However, major changes are strongly discouraged while you are in your first year of grief. Any big decisions should be carefully considered over time to avoid rash moves that may cause added regret. A year can make a big difference in how you are feeling!

Coping with Anxiety

Anxiety causes us to want to think fast and do something, so it is important to encourage yourself to just slow down. You do not need to do anything about the loss right away, so take some time to catch your breath.

- Breathe, breathe, and breathe some more. Slowing down can help you think more clearly and be less anxious.

- Engage in relaxation techniques to reduce the tension in your body.

- Get a massage or sit in a hot tub or sauna. Do activities that promote inactivity and help you relax.

- Go for a walk, paint, or listen to calming music. Color an image such as a mandala to soothe your anxiety.

- Focus on the small details instead of the bigger picture. Find detail-oriented activities to focus your attention. Try building dollhouse furniture, putting together a model airplane, doing puzzles, or even building with Legos.

- Decrease caffeine and other stimulants.

- Make small manageable decisions daily. Don't make any critical decisions (sell house, throw away belongings, etc.) at this point.
- Make a list of changes you want, and then revisit them in a week to see if you still need to make these changes.
- Make a crisis plan so you feel more prepared for a crisis.
- Pray for the peace of mind and safety of yourself and the people you care about.

Suzie's Story

Suzie lost her youngest child, her daughter, to a distracted driver who was going too fast on their residential road. The kids always played outside, they knew the rules, and there was no reason to be worried about them on the low-traffic road. When she heard a commotion, she ran out and saw her son a few doors down sitting in the middle of the road holding something, with his friends standing around him.

Suzie began questioning every decision she had made that day and wondering how she could have prevented this if she had been there. Immediately things changed in the house. Everything felt unsafe to her, and she was determined to protect her son. He was no longer allowed to play in the front yard, ride his bike, or walk to a friend's house. She wanted to know where he was at all times and watched him like a hawk. She drove him to school and picked him up. She never wanted him to be away from her. Recurrent nightmares exacerbated Suzie's anxiety. Her son never argued; he was experiencing his own grief, but with this isolation he quickly began to withdraw and become depressed. Her son was referred to a therapist by the school as his withdrawal became concerning.

During family sessions with just the two of them, Suzie's drawings always had a theme of black holes. They had a sense of controlled repetitiveness week after week. Attempts to alter her patterns or collaboratively draw were met with resistance. Challenging the validity of her restrictive behaviors through discussion was not helpful. For Suzie, the necessary insight came only when she saw her son's drawings of his family: one before his sister's death and one after her death. The "before" picture depicted a family of four smiling and standing together in front of a house on a sunny day. The "after" picture was simply the image of his mother, twice the size of him, without other objects or colors in the picture. This visual shocked her. As they talked, her son spent a lot of time describing the good times they had before his sister's death, and explained that he did not just lose her, but lost his dad and mom, too. This finally challenged Suzie's anxiety. Although she continued to be more controlling than her son wanted, Suzie began finding outlets to relax by taking a painting class and listening to books on tape. As the weather became warmer, she started taking walks around the block every evening.

Allowing feelings of anxiety to take control of your life can provide some sense of control initially. But over time this can become an all-consuming task. Constant apprehension over the future affects not only your physical health but also the other people in your life. Taking steps like spending time doing things you enjoy or simply laughing can be very helpful in reducing anxiety.

Anxiety comes from fear about what might happen. Think about some of the fears you might be experiencing after this loss.

I WORRY THAT . . .

....

....

....

....

....

....

....

....

....

....

....

....

....

....

....

Dealing with Others

Anxiety is contagious—it has a tendency to rub off on others. If you are anxious, people around you will become anxious. When faced with this anxiety, people might try to remove triggers, force you to face your fears, or show you how the fear is irrational. You do not need to rush removing your anxiety. In fact, by trying to overcome it too quickly you might actually make yourself more anxious in the process.

If anxiety compels you to make new rules for yourself and others in your life, you will be met with resistance. Your experience of the loss is causing you to react with anxiety, but not everyone else may be anxious. The rules you are implementing may not have value to others and they may be confused and even say you are overreacting. Explain your anxiety to trusted friends or a counselor, and come up with changes together.

Disbelief

"Sometimes your heart needs more time to accept what your mind already knows." —Unknown

Disbelief is one of the most easily relatable feelings right after a loss—believing people must be talking about the wrong person, for example, or that you misheard. The shock of the experience can cause you to simply not believe this is happening. Even expected losses can cause an initial shock. The denial usually fades, but for some, the disbelief may become a necessity, even a crutch. Disbelief serves a purpose by allowing you to manage your grief slowly and when you are ready. It protects you initially by diminishing the intensity of the loss. Even after denial subsides, lingering feelings of disbelief can sometimes still be present.

The shock of the event can cause you to continue as if nothing has happened, and some people may even continue their lives as if the person was still there. For example, people may continue to sleep on the same side of the bed, continue to call out to the person, expect them to walk through the door, or pretend that their spouse is simply away on a long business trip. Instances of soldiers who are pronounced dead but never return home have caused people to continue to wait for them. But the lengths to which some people try to protect themselves actually work

What Does Disbelief Look or Feel Like?

- Feeling shocked, numb, dazed, stunned, or confused
- Maintaining your life as if the person was still there
- Avoidance
- Not hearing what people are saying to you
- Disorganized thinking
- Disorientation
- Inattentiveness
- Bargaining to change the event
- Feeling like you see or hear your loved one
- Believing others are lying to you
- Paranoia or delusions

against dealing with their grief. For some, not experiencing the rituals of loss can cause a prolonged sense of disbelief.

As you are trying to make sense of the loss, you might become unaware of other things going on around you. Not hearing what people are saying, inattentiveness, disorientation, and disorganization are all common traits when you are reacting with disbelief. You are so completely focused on trying to understand the loss that you may have difficulty thinking about anything else.

Some people may begin to bargain with a higher power to change the event, believing there is a chance it was all a mistake. They might try to act in a perfect way in hopes that they will be rewarded with the ability to change the past. Others might believe they are seeing their loved one in familiar places. They might get paranoid and believe they have been lied to. With the advent of reality television, people can sometimes develop delusions of being on a reality show, responding to their loss by believing that it is all an elaborate setup and their reaction is being recorded. All these thoughts serve as a way to manage intense emotions experienced from the loss. Diminishing your disbelief will take time and patience on your part as you begin to fully understand how your loss is going to affect you. For most people, it will naturally fade as they are confronted with reality. But disbelief may also serve as a comforting way to more fully remember the person right now, so be patient.

Coping with Disbelief

When dealing with disbelief, you want to do things that are grounding. Disbelief is simply not believing the world around you, so do things that help you connect with surrounding people and places. Holding onto your denial may be the only way you still feel connected to the person, and letting it go might be extremely painful—but it is the only way to emotionally recover. If your disbelief is hindering your ability to live life, these activities can help you work through your grief:

- Participate in all of the rituals associated with the loss. You need to be given the opportunity to say goodbye.
- Even if you do not believe the loss has occurred, you can still find ways to say goodbye to the person so you can continue living your own life.
- Create a scrapbook about their life with a beginning and ending.
- Have a gathering to commemorate the person.
- Pray for strength, comfort, and clarity.
- Journal about the things you are going to miss about the person.
- Reach out to family and friends. Put someone else in charge of some responsibilities.

- Retell stories about that person. Use the person's name as often as you can when telling the story.
- Reconnect with nature and the earth. Sit in the grass and feel it, spend time listening to the waves crashing at the beach, or watch squirrels running through a park.
- Make plans for the future without the person. Take a trip, make dinner plans, or do something on your bucket list.

Oscar's Story

When little Oscar's mother became too sick to care for him, he was sent to live with his aunt. His mother had been diagnosed as HIV-positive when he was a toddler, but the family never discussed her diagnosis with him. Oscar had often gone to live with his aunt and uncle during his mother's illness, but she always came and brought him home. He was six years old when she died. No one wanted to talk to him about her death because they felt he was too young. He did not attend the funeral or clean out his old bedroom.

His aunt and uncle took him in as their own child and pretended nothing had happened. Oscar was simply told he was going to live there now and would no longer see his mother, but he was essentially on his own to figure out why. At first he thought he had done something wrong and his mother did not want to see him. As the loss continued unaddressed, he began acting out in school—going so far as to accuse his aunt and uncle of abuse—so his mother would have to come and get him. He was very confused and hurt when she didn't. Finally, the death was explained to him. But even after Oscar visited the grave, there was a part of him that continued to believe she would come back and they could go home.   →

My approach to helping Oscar involved magical thinking. When kids don't get to say goodbye, giving them a way like sending a balloon up to heaven with a note, or writing a letter and mailing it to heaven, helps give them that opportunity. In Oscar's case, he played violin so his mother could listen to his music from heaven. Even as adults, we often find it difficult to end something without official closure. Finding a way to resolve your disbelief such as attending rituals, visiting a special place, or finishing a project can all be special ways of saying goodbye after a loss.

Dealing with Others

For a while, people might try to convince you of the truth, explaining what they saw, the events that led to the loss, and how they know it to be true. People tend to be more aggressive with confronting disbelief because they see little room for interpretation—they see the loss as factual. Others may feel pressured to get you to understand the situation when decisions need to be made and they need your input. As they realize they cannot talk you out of your denial, people may become frustrated and take over your responsibilities. If you are going through a similar situation, it can be helpful to tell people that you cannot deal with these responsibilities at the moment, or explain that you need time to adapt to the changes. You might also consider putting someone you trust in charge of managing decisions for you until you feel ready.

Writing about your memories of the person can be helpful in cherishing them for who they were and what they meant to you. Take some time and think about what you remember about the person and what you think they might want you to remember.

WHEN I THINK ABOUT YOU, I THINK . . .

....

....

....

....

....

....

....

....

....

....

....

....

....

....

....

Shame

"Shame is the lie someone told you about yourself." —Anaïs Nin

Shame can develop during grief when we begin to believe that we are not only responsible for the loss, but also that we are intrinsically a bad person. Our sense of shame is developed early in our lives as we learn societal norms that tell us what makes a good person and what makes a bad person. We inadvertently shame others into following these same norms through our comments and actions about what we deem acceptable. An example we often see is body image shaming—we have been influenced by the media into thinking that if we do not look a specific way, we are not attractive.

Likewise, in grief, if we do not exhibit the "proper" reactions and emotions that are in line with people's expectations, we are prone to feel shame. Shame can limit our ability to grieve the way we need to, as it might dictate the ways in which we believe we are allowed to grieve. Some people might develop feelings of embarrassment for grieving, believing they should not be feeling the way they do, that they should be able to handle it better, or that they aren't strong enough to control their emotions.

Feelings of wanting to withdraw from society and emotionally shutting down can come from your attempts to avoid the shame you feel. Because you think your feelings are being judged by others, you might hide from others to grieve alone, or you might not want others to see you as flawed. Hiding from society can give you the opportunity to authentically feel what you need to experience.

Shame comes from a rigidity of thoughts: believing there is only one course of action, one way to feel, or one way to do things. When life does not fit into your plan, you might feel like a failure. How could you not meet your own expectations? After losing a child, many parents feel like a failure for not protecting the child, as the messages they are confronted with ask why they did not prevent it. Thoughtless statements like, "Where were you?" and "How did you let that happen?" cause an immense amount of shame.

Shame can instill a sense of worthlessness as a person. It does not matter how many wonderful things we have done in our lives, the one thing we feel shame about undoes everything else. We can become self-conscious about who we are and the choices we make, and attempt to be what the shame tells us to be. When we believe we are a bad person, we might condemn ourselves to living with pain or begin seeing suicide as an escape.

We are never all good or all bad, and it does us no good to focus on all of the perceived mistakes we have made in our lives. If you have made mistakes, they were important for you to learn from so you could grow to be a better person. We are all flawed human beings that deserve to be loved and accepted.

Coping with Shame

Some of the hardest shaming beliefs to overcome are the most difficult to share with others. Fears about what people will think about you will keep you from talking about these beliefs. It is important to identify your shame beliefs and force yourself to reject them. There is no one way to live life, and shaming beliefs only creates damaging effects to your psyche. To develop a resiliency to your shame, you must start to love yourself. And once you say these beliefs out loud and challenge what causes you to feel shame, you can be open to ask for what you need, you will feel less alone, and you can have the opportunity to begin to move forward. These are some steps you can take to challenge your self-defeating shaming beliefs:

- Social support is most important. Knowing you are not being abandoned by others because of the loss can fight self-destructive thoughts.

- Seek a grief support group to find camaraderie with others who might also be feeling shame.

- Surround yourself with friends that love and validate your feelings.

- Identify the things you do that make you a good person. Look in the mirror and tell yourself these things when you are feeling ashamed.

- Make a list of the flaws you liked about the person who is lost. Make a list of your own flaws. Remember, everyone is flawed.

- Read through your list of grievers' rights (see page 24).

- Make a list of shaming statements you have heard and reject them (see page 95 for examples of common shaming statements).

- Seek out opportunities to reflect. Meditate or pray for strength, clarity, and self-acceptance, if that is meaningful to you.

- Practice self-care. Take care of your body.

- Recognize your accomplishments. Display awards and achievements.

- Make short-term goals that you can accomplish.

- Find ways to practice altruism.

- Laugh at yourself.

What Does Shame Look or Feel Like?

- Rigid expectations about how to grieve
- Embarrassment
- Emotionally shutting down or withdrawing
- Feeling defined by the event, feeling judged by others
- Rigidity in thoughts
- Feeling like a failure
- Feeling worthless, hopeless, and self-conscious
- Lowered self-esteem
- Self-condemnation
- Suicidal ideation or attempts

Dealing with Others

We already have our own shame beliefs; do not add in or accept the beliefs of others. Avoid people who shame you. You can tell them that their statements are hurtful, but there is no way you are going to change their thoughts, and no good can come from projecting a negative self-image.

What do you need right now? It might be something emotional you need to move forward in your grief, or perhaps a new way of thinking, a concrete object, or a personal wish.

WHAT I NEED MOST IS . . .

....

....

....

....

....

....

....

....

....

....

....

....

....

....

....

....

Shaming Statements

Shaming statements are things people say to increase conformity to social norms. These types of statements are ingrained in us at a young age to teach us right from wrong, but they leave little room for flexibility. As we get older, sometimes these statements cause harm as we feel bad when we cannot or choose not to live up to the expectations. Shame defines how we act, the direction we should take in life, who we love, and how we think we should feel. Shaming beliefs are best dealt with in supportive discussions where they can be challenged as false. If you prefer to examine your shaming beliefs alone, think about the ones you hold and how they affect how you feel about yourself. Try journaling about the belief, identifying situations when it would not be true, or why the belief was important to believe at one time but does not apply anymore. Below is a list of common shaming beliefs that often prevent us from acting in ways that are true to ourselves.

- Good little boys and girls do not act that way.

- Stop acting like a baby.

- Don't be a sissy.

- No one else is complaining, so why are you?

- Women should have children.

- You'll regret that later.

- Men should be strong.

- Men should provide for their families.

- Children should never die before their parents.   →

- Let your conscience be your guide.

- You are spoiled.

- Good things happen to good people.

- You asked for it.

- Sexual feelings should be repressed, or are dirty or bad.

- If you try, you will succeed.

- No one will like you if you do that.

- Why can't you be more like them?

- You are the only one to do that.

- Mistakes are bad.

- The apple doesn't fall far from the tree.

As you can see, these beliefs are often simplistic in nature, generalizing a group or behavior instead of taking into account individual experiences, so they can easily be disputed once recognized.

Part 3

Journaling through Grief

Journaling is an effective way to express your thoughts and feelings in a safe environment. You can explore what you are truly thinking about without being judged. There is no wrong way to journal—you can write in complete sentences, short phrases, or a stream-of-consciousness style that just flows continuously. You can browse through the pages and pick out a specific prompt that you want to think about or use the blank pages at the end to write in an unguided way. You can even set a timer for five minutes and write without stopping the entire time. This will help you not to filter your thoughts and feelings and to be honest with yourself. If you wander off topic, that's fine. Let your thoughts be your guide.

THIS IS WHAT'S GOING THROUGH MY HEAD TODAY.

SOMETIMES I FEEL SO ALONE. I FEEL THAT WAY TODAY BECAUSE ...

....

....

....

....

....

....

....

....

....

....

....

....

....

....

....

....

....

....

....

OUR LAST CONVERSATION

We talked about . . .

....

....

....

....

....

....

....

....

At the time I felt . . .

....

....

....

....

....

....

....

....

I wished I had said . . .

....

....

....

....

....

....

....

....

Now I feel . . .

....

....

....

....

....

....

....

....

I WISH I HAD . . .

....

....

....

....

....

....

....

....

....

....

....

....

....

....

....

....

....

....

THE MOST PRECIOUS MEMORY I HAVE OF YOU IS . . .

....

....

....

....

....

....

....

....

....

....

....

....

....

....

....

....

....

....

I AM FEELING . . .

I LEARNED FROM YOU THAT . . .

....

....

....

....

....

....

....

....

....

....

....

....

....

....

....

....

....

....

....

I COULDN'T SLEEP TONIGHT BECAUSE I'M THINKING ABOUT . . .

....

....

....

....

....

....

....

....

....

....

....

....

....

....

....

....

....

....

....

....

I AM HURTING TODAY BECAUSE . . .

I FEEL SCARED ABOUT ...

....

....

....

....

....

....

....

....

....

....

....

....

....

....

....

....

....

....

....

I FEEL NUMB WHEN I THINK ABOUT . . .

I AM AFRAID TO . . .

....

....

....

....

....

....

....

....

....

....

....

....

....

....

....

....

....

....

....

I FEEL SO MUCH PAIN THAT I . . .

....

....

....

....

....

....

....

....

....

....

....

....

....

....

....

....

....

....

WHEN I HEARD YOU WERE GONE

I remember . . .

....

....

....

....

....

....

....

....

....

....

....

....

....

....

....

....

....

....

....

....

....

I felt . . .

AT THE MEMORIAL SERVICE, I FELT . . .

....

....

....

....

....

....

....

....

....

....

....

....

....

....

....

....

....

....

....

IT'S SO HARD TO GET OUT OF BED TODAY BECAUSE...

....

....

....

....

....

....

....

....

....

....

....

....

....

....

....

....

....

I DIDN'T JUST LOSE YOU, I LOST . . .

....

....

....

....

....

....

....

....

....

....

....

....

....

....

....

....

....

....

....

YOU MEANT A LOT TO ME...

....

....

....

....

....

....

....

....

....

....

....

....

....

....

....

....

....

....

YOU GAVE ME . . .

....

....

....

....

....

....

....

....

....

....

....

....

....

....

....

....

....

....

....

I'M SO FRUSTRATED WITH . . .

....

....

....

....

....

....

....

....

....

....

....

....

....

....

....

....

....

....

....

....

I HAD A DREAM ABOUT YOU.

It made me think about . . .

....

....

....

....

....

....

....

....

....

I woke up feeling . . .

....

....

....

....

....

....

....

....

....

TODAY I SAW . . .

I HAVE A NEW PERSPECTIVE ON LIFE. TODAY I'M GOING TO . . .

....

....

....

....

....

....

....

....

....

....

....

....

....

....

....

....

....

....

....

....

I CAN TAKE CARE OF MYSELF BY . . .

I CAN TALK TO . . .

I AM SORRY THAT . . .

....

....

....

....

....

....

....

....

....

....

....

....

....

....

....

....

....

I FEEL AT PEACE WHEN . . .

....

....

....

....

....

....

....

....

....

....

....

....

....

....

....

....

....

....

I FEEL GRATEFUL FOR . . .

....

....

....

....

....

....

....

....

....

....

....

....

....

....

....

....

....

....

I HAVE CHANGED BECAUSE . . .

....

....

....

....

....

....

....

....

....

....

....

....

....

....

....

....

....

....

....

I CAN LOOK FORWARD TO . . .

WHEN I THINK ABOUT THE FUTURE . . .

I see . . .

....

....

....

....

....

....

....

....

....

I look like . . .

....

....

....

....

....

....

....

....

....

I live . . .

....

....

....

....

....

....

....

....

....

The people in my life are . . .

....

....

....

....

....

....

....

....

....

I HOPE TO LEARN . . .

....

....

....

....

....

....

....

....

....

....

....

....

....

....

....

....

....

....

WHEN SOMEONE ASKS ME ABOUT YOU, I WILL TELL THEM . . .

DEAR GRIEF,

....

....

....

....

....

....

....

....

....

....

....

....

....

....

....

....

....

....

....

....

Open Journal

As You Move On

"In three words I can sum up everything I know about life—it goes on." —Robert Frost

Inevitably when people grieve, they wonder when they will feel normal again. What they are asking is when they will stop missing the person, when they can be their old self again, and when life will return to the five minutes before they heard about the loss. I always ask, "What is normal?" Your grief is normal. You will always miss the person—and that is normal. And it is normal to wish to go back to a simpler time.

Everyone grieves at their own pace and in their own way, and everyone learns something different from it. After a loss, you can feel fragmented as you transition from a time in your life when you had the person, to a time when they are no longer with you. You may have lost your direction, your sense of who you are, and your sense of stability. You will regain those, but in a different way. Life experiences are lessons, which if we take the opportunity to learn from, can lead us to a richer, fuller life. One family who lost their infant daughter went on to call her "our teacher," because they recognized that she taught them so many lessons, including how to appreciate each other, value life, and not get swept up in the small stuff.

Integrating your loss means that you can take this life experience, allow it to be a part of who you are now, and begin to feel whole again. Your experience might encourage you to become more cautious, realizing you are not invincible. You might begin to cherish the little things more often, or start living in the present instead of always looking toward the future. This experience might make you realize how hard you are on yourself, always reaching to meet unattainable standards instead of just loving yourself for who you are. Perhaps the experience of loss will cause you to realize your own limitations in life. These are not bad changes. These shifts in how you see the world represent how you are being transformed, how you incorporate your loss, and how it teaches you. Your loss will change you forever, but my hope is that your grief will not control your life—that instead, you can see that the person you lost is a part of the person you are now.

As we end this book, I want to share a few hopes that I have for you. I hope you will continue your journey of self-awareness and growth. Learning from life and becoming cognizant of who you are in the world is a wise and rewarding way to proceed. I hope you continue to make room in your heart for love. Love yourself and accept love from others. I hope you find a way to make your loss a part of who you are, but not the definition of who you are. And lastly, I hope you have found some comfort and direction in the stories and advice I've shared, so that you do not feel so alone in your grief, and you know that each step you take is leading you toward a future with promise, however unknown.

Appendix

NORMAL GRIEF VERSUS CLINICAL DEPRESSION

When you're grieving, it is commonplace to use the word *depression* to communicate feelings of sadness. The word depression though is a clinical term describing a prolonged sadness that causes significant impairment in your ability to function in either your social, personal, or work life. A loss may initially disrupt your ability to function in the normal grieving process, but prolonged impairment is a sign that you might need some help to navigate your grief.

To help you better understand the difference between the experiences of grief and depression, the table on the following pages compares normal grief and the definition of clinical depression as defined by the *Diagnostic and Statistical Manual of Mental Disorders (DSM)*.

If the descriptions in the left category, "Signs of Normal Grief," are more descriptive of your experience, it is likely that you are going through healthy grief and should expect to continue to heal over time. If you relate to one or more of the descriptions on the right, "Signs of Clinical Depression," you could be suffering from something more serious, and should speak with a doctor or mental health professional. Even if you do not feel you are clinically depressed, but simply feel stuck in your grief, unsupported, or just want to talk to someone, it is often helpful to find a mental health professional.

Signs of Normal Grief	Signs of Clinical Depression
Experience of the loss has not caused noticeable impairment to your daily functioning. Although you are experiencing grief, you are able to take care of your basic needs.	Loss is causing a noticeable change from previous functioning. For example, you are unable to work, be with other people, or take care of yourself.
Feeling sad throughout the day, but have times when you are happy. The amount of time during each day that you are feeling sad is generally decreasing.	Depressed mood throughout most of the day, nearly every day. Intrusive thoughts about your loved one.
Able to engage in activities of interest or pleasure. Continue to have a social group on which you can rely.	Diminished interest or pleasure in all, or almost all, activities. Avoiding things that cause you to think about the loss. Avoiding interactions with friends or family.
Maintaining current levels of health and weight.	Significant weight loss when not dieting, or weight gain. A change of more than 5% of body weight in a month.
Able to concentrate on a task when needed.	Diminished ability to think or concentrate or indecisiveness nearly every day.

Signs of Normal Grief	Signs of Clinical Depression
Able to sleep at night. Following sleep routines. Able to get out of bed in the morning and maintain daily tasks.	Insomnia or excessive sleepiness nearly every day. Regularly using medications to induce sleep. Chronic nightmares or restlessness thinking about the loss.
Able to engage in relaxation techniques. Able to complete tasks of daily living. Able to engage in physical tasks when required without accidents.	Anxiety-related nervous habits like pacing, fidgeting, wringing hands. Increased incidents of tripping, falling, bumping into things.
Energetic enough to exert yourself to complete tasks.	Fatigue or loss of energy nearly every day.
Able to express feelings about the loss, and feelings do not cause you to feel badly about yourself.	Feelings of worthlessness or excessive or inappropriate guilt nearly every day. Excessive anger or bitterness about the loss.
Some thoughts about death, suicide, and wanting to join the person (these feelings can be normal).	Persistently recurring thoughts of death, recurrent suicidal ideation, suicide attempt, or specific plan for committing suicide.

Resources

Many resources are available to help those who are grieving a loss. I often utilize hospice organizations because they maintain their own groups and facilities and keep updated information for your specific area. You might also consider asking for assistance from your local hospital, place of worship, or funeral director in finding the support you need. Below are some of my favorite resources.

PODCAST

What's Your Grief?

Eleanor Haley and Litsa Williams maintain a website and podcast that are useful during times of grief. They are great at normalizing the experience of grief by sharing their own stories and providing useful tips. Their website is Whatsyourgrief.com and their podcast can be found on iTunes under the title "What's Your Grief?"

BOOKS

Kübler-Ross, Elisabeth, and David Kessler. *Life Lessons*. New York: Scribner, 2000.

Kübler-Ross, Elisabeth, and David Kessler. *On Grief and Grieving*. New York: Scribner, 2005.

McCracken, Anne, and Mary Semel. *A Broken Heart Still Beats: After Your Child Dies*. Center City, MN: Hazelden, 1998.

Noel, Brook, and Pamela D. Blair. *I Wasn't Ready to Say Goodbye: Surviving, Coping and Healing after the Sudden Death of a Loved One*. Naperville, IL: Sourcebooks, 2008.

Prashant, Lyn. *The Art of Transforming Grief: Degriefing Counseling and Education*. San Anselmo, CA: L. Prashant, 2002.

Schoeneck, Therese S., and Kathleen Jacques. *Hope for Bereaved: Understanding, Coping, and Growing through Grief.* Syracuse, NY: Hope for Bereaved, 2001.

Williams, Mark, John Teasdale, Zindel Segal, and Jon Kabat-Zinn. *The Mindful Way through Depression.* New York: The Guilford Press, 2007.

Wolfelt, Alan D. *Healing Your Grieving Heart: 100 Practical Ideas.* Fort Collins, CO: Companion, 2001.

Wolfelt, Alan D. *Healing Your Holiday Grief: 100 Practical Ideas for Blending Mourning and Celebration During the Holiday Season.* Fort Collins, CO: Companion, 2005.

Wolfelt, Alan D. *The Journey through Grief: Reflections on Healing.* Fort Collins, CO: Companion, 1997.

WEBSITES AND ORGANIZATIONS

AARP

Online resources, AARP Grief and Loss Programs
AARP Grief and Loss Programs
601 E Street, NW
Washington, DC 20049
202-434-2260
aarp.org

American Foundation for Suicide Prevention

Resources for those affected by or contemplating suicide.
120 Wall Street, 29th floor
New York, NY 10005
888-333-AFSP (2377)
afsp.org

Association for Death Education and Counseling

Resources for those experiencing grief including seminars, counselors, and end-of-life planning.

One Parkview Plaza, Suite 800
Oakbrook Terrace, IL 60181
847-686-2240
adec.org

The Compassionate Friends

Support for bereaved families after the death of a child.

1000 Jorie Blvd. Suite 140
Oak Brook, IL 60523
630-990-0010; 877-969-0010 (toll-free)
compassionatefriends.org

The Daily Motivator by Ralph Marston

Provides free daily meditations online or by paid subscription through email.
greatday.com

The Dougy Center

The National Center for Grieving Children and Families. Resources and group support for children and families experiencing grief.

PO Box 86852
Portland, OR 97286
866-775-5683
dougy.org

Grief Net

An Internet community of people dealing with grief, death, and loss.

PO Box 3272
Ann Arbor, MI 48106
griefnet.org

Grief Recovery after Substance Passing (GRASP)

Resources for survivors of a loss due to substance abuse or addiction.

8502 E. Chapman Avenue #156
Orange, CA 92869
714-865-7879
grasphelp.org

Grief Share

Online support and grief support group.
PO Box 1739
Wake Forest, NC 27588
800-395-5755
griefshare.org

Hello Grief

Online community to share and learn about grief and loss.
hellogrief.org

Hope for Bereaved

Support for those grieving, newsletter, and community education programs.
4500 Onondaga Blvd
Syracuse, NY 13219
315-475-HOPE (4673)
hopeforbereaved.com

Hospice Foundation

Resources for those experiencing a loss, end-of-life care, help locating
your local hospice.
1710 Rhode Island Ave, NW, Suite 400
Washington, DC 20036
202-457-5811/800-854-3402
hospicefoundation.org

National Suicide Prevention Lifeline

Free and confidential support to people in suicidal crisis or emotional distress
24 hours a day, 7 days a week.
1-800-273-TALK (8255)
suicidepreventionlifeline.org

SLAP'D (Surviving Life after a Parent Dies)

Online forum for teenagers and young adults who are grieving the loss of a parent.
slapd.com

The Sudden Unexplained Death in Childhood Foundation (SUDC Foundation)

Information, support, and counseling to those who have experienced the unexplained death of a child.

549 Pompton Avenue, Suite 197

Cedar Grove, NJ 07009

sudc.org

Sri Chinmoy Centre

Provides meditation classes and inspirational stories.

srichinmoycentre.org

References

American Psychiatric Association. *Diagnostic and Statistical Manual of Mental Disorders*. 4th ed. Washington, DC: American Psychiatric Association, 2000.

Becker, Ernest. *The Denial of Death*. New York: The Free Press, 1973.

Burroughs, Augusten. *This Is How*. New York: St. Martin's Press, 2012.

Deits, Bob. *Life after Loss*. Cambridge, MA: Da Capo Press, 2009.

Feifel, Herman and Vivian T. Nagy. "Another Look at Fear of Death." *Journal of Consulting and Clinical Psychology*. 49, no. 2 (1981): 278–286.

Feifel, Herman. "Psychology and the Death-Awareness Movement." *Journal of Clinical Child Psychology*. 3, no. 2 (1974): 6–7.

Gravitz, Herbert L., and Julie D. Bowden. *Recovery: A Guide for Adult Children of Alcoholics*. New York: Simon and Schuster, Inc., 1987.

Grof, Stanislov, and Joan Halifax. *The Human Encounter with Death*. New York: E.P. Dutton, 1977.

Katon, Wayne, Evette Ludman, Gregory E. Simon, Elizabeth Lin, Mark Sullivan, Edward Walker, Terry Bush, et al. *The Depression Helpbook*. Boulder, Colorado: Bull Publishing Company, 2008.

Kosminsky, Phyllis. *Getting Back to Life When Grief Won't Heal*. New York: McGraw Hill, 2007.

Kübler-Ross, Elisabeth and David Kessler. *Life Lessons*. New York: Scribner, 2000.

Kübler-Ross, Elisabeth and David Kessler. *On Grief and Grieving*. New York: Scribner, 2005.

Lukas, Christopher and Seiden, Henry M. *Silent Grief Living in the Wake of Suicide*. Philadelphia: Jessica Kingsley Publishers, 2007.

Maurer, Adah. "Maturation of Concepts of Death." *British Journal of Medical Psychology*. 39 (1966):35–41.

Mazlow, Abraham. *Toward a Psychology of Being.* New York: Van Nostrand, 1968.

McCracken, Anne, and Mary Semel. *A Broken Heart Still Beats: After Your Child Dies.* Center City, MN: Hazelden, 1998.

Mims, Cedric. *When We Die. The Science, Culture, and Rituals of Death.* St. Martin's Press: New York, 1998.

Noel, Brook, and Pamela D. Blair. *I Wasn't Ready to Say Goodbye: Surviving, Coping and Healing after the Sudden Death of a Loved One.* Naperville, IL: Sourcebooks, 2008.

Prashant, Lyn. *The Art of Transforming Grief: Degriefing Counseling and Education.* San Anselmo, CA: L. Prashant, 2002.

Schoeneck, Therese S., and Kathleen Jacques. *Hope for Bereaved: Understanding, Coping, and Growing through Grief.* Syracuse, NY: Hope for Bereaved, 2001.

Stevenson, Robert G., and Eileen P. Stevenson. *Teaching Students About Death: A Comprehensive Resource for Educators and Parents.* Philadelphia: The Charles Press, 1996.

Williams, Mark, John Teasdale, Zindel Segal, and Jon Kabat-Zinn. *The Mindful Way through Depression.* New York: The Guilford Press, 2007.

Wolfelt, Alan D. *Understanding Grief: Helping Yourself Heal.* New York: Brunner-Routledge, 1992.

Wolfelt, Alan D. *Healing a Friend's Grieving Heart: 100 Practical Ideas for Helping Someone You Love through Loss.* Fort Collins, CO: Companion, 2001.

Wolfelt, Alan D. *Healing Your Grieving Heart: 100 Practical Ideas: Compassionate Advice and Simple Activities to Help You through Your Loss.* Fort Collins: Companion, 2001.

Wolfelt, Alan D. *Healing Your Holiday Grief: 100 Practical Ideas for Blending Mourning and Celebration during the Holiday Season.* Fort Collins, CO: Companion, 2005.

Wolfelt, Alan D. *The Journey through Grief: Reflections on Healing.* Fort Collins, CO: Companion, 1997.

Index

Acknowledgments

I would like to thank those who have supported me through my experiences of grief to be able to become more fully aware to help others, those who have shared their journey through grief with me throughout the years, and most importantly my husband who, without his ongoing support and understanding, I could not be there for others.